Croner's Guide to Managing Redundancy

**Lynda Jay
and
Bob Patchett**

Croner Publications Ltd
Croner House
London Road
Kingston upon Thames
Surrey KT2 6SR
Telephone: 0181-547 3333

Published by
Croner Publications Ltd
Croner House
London Road
Kingston upon Thames
Surrey KT2 6SR
Tel: 0181-547 3333

While every care has been taken
in the writing and editing of this book,
readers should be aware that only Acts of Parliament
and Statutory Instruments have the force of law,
and that only the courts can authoritatively
interpret the law.

British Library Cataloguing-in-Publication Data.
A catalogue record for this book
is available from the British Library.

ISBN 1 85524 127 7

Printed by Whitstable Litho Printers Ltd, Whitstable, Kent.

Contents

Introduction   1

1   Avoiding Redundancy   5

Introduction
Planning to Obviate Redundancy
Alternative Labour Cost Reduction Actions

2   Short-time Working and Lay-off   19

Introduction
Contractual Provision
Guarantee Payments
Entitlement to a Redundancy Payment

3   Consultation with Trade Unions   23

Introduction
Recognised Trade Unions
The Consultation Process
Consulting with Non-unionised Employees
Notifying the Department of Employment

4   Defining Dismissal   29

Introduction
Dismissal by the Employer
Fixed-term Contract Expires
Constructive Dismissal
Failure to Allow Return from Maternity Leave
Dismissals that Qualify for Redundancy Payments

Terminations of Contracts that do not Qualify for
    Redundancy Payments
Common Questions

5   Defining Redundancy   45

Introduction
The Closure of the Business
"In the Place of Work"
Requirements for Work of a Particular Kind
What is "Work of a Particular Kind"?
Unfair Redundancy — Unsound Reasons
Next Step…

6   Establishing Fair Selection   57

Introduction
What is an Undertaking?
Who are Employees in Similar Positions?
What are the Inadmissible Reasons?
Selection Criteria
Claims of Discrimination with Collective Agreements
Consultation
Appeals Procedure
Common Questions

7   A Reasonable Procedure   73

Introduction
Consultation with the Individual Employee
Why the Emphasis on Consultation?
Suitable Alternative Employment
Transferred Redundancy
The Legal Remedies
Common Questions

8 Minimising the Impact   **87**

Introduction
Encouraging Volunteers
Alternatives to Unemployment
Helping the Employees

9 Redundancy Payments   **97**

Introduction
Exceptions
Redundancy Pay
Continuous Employment
The Legal Remedy
Common Questions

Glossary   **119**

Useful Addresses   **127**

Appendix 1 — Guarantee Payments   **131**

Appendix 2 — Calculating Qualifying Service   **135**

Appendix 3 — Exclusions from the Right to Claim Unfair Dismissal   **141**

Appendix 4 — Interim Relief   **143**

Appendix 5 — Insolvency   **145**

Appendix 6 — Notification to the   **149**
                         Employment Department

Appendix 7 — Time Off   **155**

Further Information   **157**

Index   **161**

Introduction

Unfortunately, there can be few organisations today that have managed to avoid making redundancies at some stage.

The managers who have to deal with these difficult situations have the added burden of working their way through a vast amount of employment legislation and case law. The law concerning redundancy is diverse, complex and subject, or so it seems, to constant change.

Redundancy payments were established as a statutory right almost 30 years ago, and a succession of UK Governments and the EU have developed a complicated web of individual and collective rights.

Croner's Guide to Managing Redundancy aims to summarise the law clearly and concisely, to highlight the pitfalls and to point out the common misconceptions.

The guide also contains helpful information on measures to avoid redundancies and how to minimise their impact on all concerned.

Managing redundancy will never be simple or straightforward, but it is hoped this book will enable managers to work through redundancies more effectively, and to succeed at tribunal if this becomes necessary.

The Scope of the Book

To do this the book is divided into nine chapters.

Chapter 1: Avoiding Redundancy

This describes management techniques for minimising the likelihood of redundancy, considers options for avoiding redundancy and finally looks at alternatives to redundancy if payroll costs must be reduced.

Chapter 2: Short-time Working and Lay-off

An employee who is put on short-time working or laid off may qualify for the right to a guarantee payment and also to a redundancy payment. Details are included in this chapter to help the employer to decide on the appropriate action to take.

Chapter 3: Consultation with Trade Unions

Quite apart from the requirement to consult with individuals, UK law demands that employers consult collectively with their recognised trade unions. We describe how employers should best tackle this difficult area.

Chapter 4: Defining Dismissal

A dismissal on the grounds of redundancy involves consideration of a complicated mix of statutory and contractual entitlements. We lead you through the legalistic maze!

Chapter 5: Defining Redundancy

Once you have defined dismissal we help you to define redundancy!

Chapter 6: Establishing Fair Selection

When some employees are dismissed and others retained, the redundant employees can challenge the method of selection. We guide you through the maze.

Chapter 7: A Reasonable Procedure

It is often said that employees who are consulted are more likely to react in a constructive way and may be able to suggest alternatives to redundancy. We help you through this difficult area.

Chapter 8: Minimising the Impact

Although redundancy may be inevitable, there is a great deal the employer can do to minimise the impact on employees. We lead you through each option in turn.

Chapter 9: Redundancy Payments

Finally the book deals with redundancy payments — what to pay and when.

Before going further into this book, two important points must be borne in mind. First, even where redundancy is governed by legislation, individual companies and organisations will still have their own policies and procedures. Second, it is impossible, given the length of this book — and incompatible with its purpose — to quote chapter and verse of statutes and case law. Further details can be obtained from the Department of Employment, the Advisory Conciliation and Arbitration Service (ACAS) or from *Croner's Reference Book for Employers*.

1   Avoiding Redundancy

Introduction

This chapter describes management techniques for minimising the likelihood of redundancy, considers options for avoiding redundancy if business performance begins to deteriorate, and finally looks at alternatives to redundancy if payroll costs must be reduced.

Planning to Obviate Redundancy

Redundancy is brought about either by a business crisis or by poor manpower planning. Crises such as the loss of a large contract or failure of a major debtor require a prompt reaction which may well include redundancy, though alternatives are explored later in this chapter. However, too often redundancy results from a gradual build-up of problems. In a recession sales fall, then margins are reduced, cost increases are resisted, but cost reducing actions are taken too late to balance the books; an appallingly high wages bill makes redundancy irresistible. Whilst the cause of the business problem lies outside the company, the management problem results from poor organisational housekeeping — inadequate manpower planning. Many companies recognise this in hindsight and have the good sense to install simple but sound manpower planning systems to avoid, or at least minimise, the trauma of redundancy in the future.

Manpower Planning

Effective manpower planning is a natural offshoot from business planning. The process is as follows.

1. Forecast future business over the coming 10 years — in great detail for one year, in detail for the next four years and in outline for the remaining five years.

2. Produce corresponding business plans for dealing with forecasted business requirements.

3. Translate the business plans into manpower forecasts, ie how many people will be needed, what jobs and when. Clearly both business plans and manpower forecasts must remain dynamic documents that are altered to meet inevitable changes in business forecasts.

4. Compare the existing staffing structure with the manpower forecasts. Allow for losses such as retirements and normal labour turnover.

5. At appropriate points in the future identify the gaps between the manpower forecasts and the anticipated staffing structure. A positive gap is a labour shortage which must be filled either by recruiting externally or by redeploying existing staff. A negative gap shows a surplus of manpower of a certain type.

6. Action to avoid redundancy means taking all practicable steps to use this surplus manpower to meet any positive recruitment needs, for example:

   (a) agree with all employees, especially those directly affected, that they will transfer to the alternative work as their own jobs disappear — deal in advance with any contractual considerations

   (b) provide training for existing employees when they are redeployed

   (c) at an appropriate time call in external trainers to teach groups of existing employees skills they will, or may, need to fulfil the needs of the manpower forecast; this may be to equip them for specific new jobs, to enable them to absorb changes in their existing jobs or to make them generally more competent and thus more flexible

   (d) for similar reasons offer incentives, such as a refund of fees or day release, to appropriate employees to attend long-term college courses or to make use of distance-learning materials

(e) where appropriate redeploy staff into new jobs as these are created, and engage people on temporary contracts to see out the disappearing jobs.

Core Staffing

A planning system which takes redundancy avoidance a stage further involves a combination of "zero-base planning" with the greatest possible reduction in the size of the core staff. Core staff are those in jobs which are critical regardless of the size of the business load. It works as follows.

1. Use business forecasts to predict the lowest level of business that is anticipated or that could be sustained.

2. Determine accurately the staffing requirements to meet this lowest level of business. At this stage ignore completely current staffing structures and levels; to be absolutely sure ignore current systems — how things are done — though this clearly will require wider senior staff involvement. This minimal requirement defines your core staff.

3. Plan how to increase manpower to meet higher-than-minimum business levels. For short-term peaks you may use overtime or agency staff. However, for longer upturns you should plan to recruit people on temporary contracts. Given time — which is the essence of planning — people may be found to undertake almost any form of work, from labourer to chief executive. Many people, through lifestyle or financial or other business circumstances, are content to work occasionally. You may have to advertise, engage agencies or use business contacts to locate potential staff. When they are found, you should explain the situation fully to them — there would be no guarantees either side. You then have a register of suitable people who may be called upon at short notice.

4. As business drops off, you may then lay off the temporary staff. They are entitled to the notification and consultation rights explained later in this book, and to a redundancy payment and protection against unfair selection for dismissal if they have two or more years' service. Technically you have redundancy, yet without the trauma for either party.

5. This system works as explained if you are starting a business on a green field site. If you have a workforce already you need to retain your zero-based plan and relate to it every personnel decision governing recruitment and so on, such that you approach the plan as closely and as soon as is practicable.

Two considerations are vitally important when making and implementing manpower plans. First, take full account of employees' statutory and contractual rights. A temporary contract must be described accordingly and indicate the probable duration of employment. A contract for a specific job or set of duties may not be changed unilaterally. Temporary employees acquire many statutory rights immediately, such as protection against discrimination and the right to join or not join a trade union and take part in its activities. Other rights accrue after two years' service, eg to receive a redundancy payment or not to be unfairly dismissed. Statutory notice rights increase annually.

The second consideration is to involve recognised trade unions in the earliest stages of planning. The less they are involved, the more suspicious they will be of the motives, and the more resistant they will be to the plans. The aim in this exercise is to avoid redundancy and to give the greatest security of employment to the employees — their members — which is a key trade union aim. Core staffing gives probably the greatest practicable degree of job security available. Therefore if you are open and honest with your trade unions you inevitably will harness their support and persuasive powers to achieve your aims.

Reviewing the Business to Avoid Redundancy

Even if redundancy seems probable, avoid a knee-jerk reaction. Take a calm and objective review of the position, and consider the following questions.

1. Is the downturn likely to be permanent or temporary and, if the latter, for how long?

   Redundancy has a permanence — it is difficult to re-employ and motivate staff you have made redundant, and why pay out redundancy compensation to people you may need to employ again? Conversely, it is better to face the reality of a permanent downturn sooner rather than later, if only to bring forward the cost saving exercise. Organisations can survive one redundancy exercise, however savage, but a series of smaller exercises, resulting from failure to recognise the size of the business problem, can cause chaos to systems and thoroughly demotivate the workforce.

   Determine the size of the business problem before considering redundancy.

2. When reviewing options for dealing with temporary business downturns, explore a range of scenarios. Looking from the smallest to the largest volume of redundancies, compare the cost of redundancy, ie statutory redundancy pay, notice pay and any *ex gratia* payments, with the cost of maintaining staff in employment, albeit doing different work.

   Put more simply: calculate the total cost of redundancy and divide it by the total weekly cost of employing the people affected. The resulting figure is the number of weeks into the future when cost savings will begin, assuming remaining staff will cope satisfactorily with the remaining work. In the meantime costs are continuing with, perhaps, a reduction in productivity — and your cash flow will suffer from the lump sum payments.

   Consider and cost a range of options before making your decision.

3. Why is the business suffering? Is it technological
    change? Are the customers' needs changing? Are you no
    longer as good as your competitors? Unless you can give
    authoritative answers to these questions, you could use
    consultants to help you frame appropriate areas to
    examine. Implementing redundancy to produce a leaner
    and fitter organisation is healthy; as a response to
    failure, it compounds the failure.

    Ensure that you know precisely the reason for your
    difficulties; only then can you tackle them efficiently.

4. If you are suffering from low volume of orders, is it
    because the business is disappearing or because it is
    harder to find? If it is the latter, then consider making a
    concentrated drive to find it. A strategic decision should
    be made as to whether to focus on the existing customer
    base and press for higher volumes, or for a broader
    uptake of your products if you have a variety of these or
    to concentrate on finding new customers.

    If redundancy is in the air, then some of your most
    enthusiastic salespeople are your non-sales employees.
    They will need some training, though many of them will
    already have sound product knowledge, customer
    understanding and enthusiasm. They will need excellent
    and readily available back-up so that decisions may be
    taken quickly. They may then need little more than a
    telephone and Yellow Pages. The regular sales staff
    could be targeted more accurately towards high
    potential new business.

    If at least some demand remains in the market, go all
    out to meet it. Companies have made tremendous leaps
    out of recession by harnessing the intelligence and
    enthusiasm of their accountants, personnel officers,
    ledger clerks, toolmakers, supervisors and other staff.

5. Is there business to be had in different markets? Ask the
    following questions:

    • What plant do we have, and what else can it produce
      or be used for? Can we use our printing machines to

produce packing for local companies? Or sell spare capacity in our machine shop to other engineers?

- What skills do we have? Could not our export section persuade recession-hit companies to use their services to trade abroad? Could our wages or computer sectors handle other companies' payrolls or annual tax returns?

- What knowledge do we have? Could our sales department handle the whole sales operations of other companies? Or our personnel department look after other local companies?

Identify the strengths within the company and look to apply them in new areas. This exercise may be enough to see you through a difficult patch, but could also open up permanent profit generating activities.

6. Often during recession companies recognise that they are under-employing some of their expensive experts. Take the opportunity of hiring them out. The employees will be invigorated, are likely to gain useful experience and should be able to bring in considerably more than their cost to you. Similarly offer out teams of people such as your buildings maintenance crew, programmers, training team or credit managers. You will need to reassure them about what you are doing, ie offering them as expert consultants, not surplus staff, and must take care of any contract and insurance arrangements.

Identify expensive staff who are under-utilised and look outside the organisation to find ways of having them earn at least their cost to you.

7. Finally in this section about reviewing the business — why not involve employees?

- They have a vested interest in avoiding redundancy.

- Because you are showing them respect, they will feel motivated to help.

- They are far more likely to go along with your suggestions for survival.

- Inviting their help is a gentle way of introducing to them the possibility of redundancy and, if redundancy becomes necessary, they are likely to be less resistant.

- They have between them a lot of skill, experience, knowledge and intelligence which, properly tapped, could produce excellent suggestions for resolving current difficulties.

Selling the Business

Closing down a business is an expensive exercise. The costs do not end when the last person to leave puts out the light and locks the door. Therefore an owner who wishes to divest him or herself of a business is likely to look for a buyer. Although the business may be losing money, it may still be more attractive to potential buyers if it is still trading with an existing network of suppliers and customers and, most importantly, a team of people who know how things work.

Therefore, there is much to be said for continuing to trade and keeping the workforce. However, the extent of trading losses and the state of the market for business acquisitions might require the owner to restrict the scale of business to the more profitable areas and, as a last resort, to pare down the staff to the essentials.

If the business is sold, employees are given certain protection by the **Transfer of Undertaking Regulations (TUPE) 1981**:

- they may not be dismissed as a result of the transfer unless valid economic, technical or organisational reasons necessitate a change in the workforce

- their contracts are transferred intact except for pension provisions; this means that their wages, holiday and other entitlements may not be changed without their agreement

- if the business is to retain a separate identity, recognition of an independent trade union will continue, as will any agreements made with that union
- information about the transfer and its effect on employees must be given to any recognised unions far enough in advance for them to consider and make their representations to the employer, and
- the employer must consult with the recognised union and try to seek agreement on proposals for dealing with the employees.

Management Buy-outs

Frequently, ailing businesses are bought by employees, or more usually by managers who see the problems and believe they be can resolved profitably. In many instances the company, whilst not ailing greatly, has not fitted comfortably into the portfolio of its corporate owner, who has been content to sell it off.

However, the buying managers may have to make a heavy personal financial commitment, and have to convince banks both that they have a viable business and that they have the knowledge and skill to make it profitable. Examination of would-be owner-managers is thorough and intense.

A management buy-out, by reviving an ailing business, can obviate redundancy of the whole workforce. However, the potential owners may have to carry out some redundancies in order to make the business viable and thus attract capital.

Alternative Labour Cost Reduction Actions

If redundancy appears inevitable, there is a legal obligation to notify and consult with employees and their representatives: this is explained in a later chapter. However, the wise employer will consult with employees anyway in order to gain their understanding of the situation, test their reaction to proposals, draw out any ideas they may have to help resolve the problem and seek their co-operation in doing whatever appears necessary.

Redundancy is a threat to employees, however if some basic psychology is utilised — such as if you threaten me, I will resist; if you share your problem with me, I will want to help resolve it — this may improve negotiations.

Some of the following options may be tabled to employees for discussions, or it may be judged more prudent to put redundancy on the table and lead employees gently to these alternatives.

Bring Forward Holidays

If the crisis is likely to be short, or if more time is needed to work on the problem, encourage employees to bring forward their holidays. This has little immediate effect on costs, but removes from the site people who would have little useful work to do, reduces the drain on resources and would keep any stock levels low.

This action is effective and only requires acceptance by the people concerned.

Reduction in Wages

Generally speaking, some employees given a choice would choose a 10% reduction in wages rather than a 10% redundancy situation. However, this option must be played carefully since it may not be so attractive to employees who would receive a large redundancy payment or who might expect to get other work quickly.

The option would involve a change to an essential element of the employment contract; if handled badly it could lead to successful claims of constructive dismissal. Therefore offer it clearly as a suggested alternative and not a threat, allow for ample consultation and gain the agreement of the employees affected. However if, after full consultation, all but a very small minority of employees accept the wage reduction as an alternative to redundancy, it is possible that this minority may fail in any claim for constructive dismissal or maintenance of the old wage. Nonetheless, this may be a perilous situation: try to avoid it at all costs.

Link Pay to Business Performance

If wages are reduced to meet a decline in business performance, staff are likely to be tolerant for a long time as long as the recession continues. However, the first whiff of business improvement will, understandably, have them looking to end the sacrifice and revert to the old wage levels. A formula for signalling and implementing this move would obviate resentment, keep the lid on employee relations and probably help gain acceptance for the wage reduction in the first place.

The formula might be a simple threshold — eg when we return to the previous year's level of orders in two consecutive months, old wage levels will be reintroduced. On the other hand a stepped formula might be more appropriate — eg an $x\%$ rise in monthly or quarterly profit will trigger a $y\%$ increase on the reduced wage levels.

This approach can be a reassuring one for employees who are being asked to share in the employer's misfortunes or who are attempting to avoid redundancy. For this reason it would be wrong to apply it if business is unlikely to recover.

Reduce Hours

The emphasis in this option is to reduce hours to match available work, with a corresponding reduction in wages. It is discussed in detail in Chapter 2.

Invite Volunteers for Part-time Work

Employees with long service might welcome an opportunity to work shorter hours, albeit with a lower income, because they may desire more leisure time, relief from stress or an opportunity to sample self-employment through a paying hobby such as stamp-dealing or garden design. A secure job in difficult times and a secure pension are great antidotes to these fantasies, but if this security is threatened, the alternatives by comparison appear to be less risky.

Any employees with such ambitions may be happy to come to an arrangement and thereby save part of their salary. It may be that the job already carries spare capacity; perhaps their own motivation might enable them to perform all their important duties in fewer hours, or some reshuffling of duties may need to happen.

Job Sharing

This is an extension of the part-time working concept whereby two people, each working part-time, carry out one job. Employee A may work from 9.00 am until 1.30 pm, and employee B from 1.00 pm until 5.30 pm — giving a 30 minute period for handover if this is necessary. Alternatively the split could be on days so that each employee works, say, two days one week and three days the next. Because of employee fixed costs and pay for any handover periods a split job could cost a little more than a single employee. However, there is ample evidence that personal performance increases as hours are reduced, thus the productivity of the job is likely to increase. Also there is cover, if required, for lunch breaks and perhaps even holidays and sickness absence. Effective management requires that the joint job-holders have clear common aims and standards.

Job sharing is a useful working arrangement which operates successfully even at senior levels, for example in the Civil Service. In the context of avoiding redundancy it is a means of reducing the number of jobs to match work demand without necessarily reducing employees by the same number. Clearly it is applicable only with the full agreement of the employees concerned.

These are examples of arrangements that the employer may consider as alternatives to redundancy. Their suitability will depend upon the particular business circumstances, whether the lower level of business or profitability is likely to be short term or permanent, and the relations with the employees.

When introducing them as possible alternatives to redundancy, take care to consult fully with recognised trade unions and with individual employees affected. Avoid giving or suggesting a guarantee that there will be no redundancy and monitor carefully any rearranged work patterns to ensure that they achieve the desired aims.

In the next chapter we look in more detail at the issues of short-time working and lay-offs.

2 Short-time Working and Lay-off

Introduction

An employee who is put on short-time working or laid off, as defined by s.87(1) and (2) of the **Employment Protection (Consolidation) Act 1978** (EP(C)A), may qualify for the right to a guarantee payment and also to a redundancy payment.

Definitions of Key Terms

Short-time working

The legal definition of short-time working is when as a result of a reduction in work, the employee's weekly pay falls below half the normal weekly rate.

Lay-off

If the employee's remuneration depends on the provision of work, and in any week there is no entitlement to remuneration because no work is provided, then that week is a week of lay-off.

A week

A week is determined by the day on which weekly pay is paid. It runs from Sunday to Saturday, unless weekly pay is not calculated with Saturday as the last day of the week, in which case the week ends on that day.

Contractual Provision

There must be either an express term or an implied term of the contract (ie established by custom and practice). If the contract of employment does not allow the employer discretion to put an employee on short-time working or to lay off, and the employee does not consent to this, then the employer risks a breach of contract claim for monies unpaid, or an action under the **Wages Act 1986**, and possibly a constructive dismissal claim as well.

Guarantee Payments

If employees are on short-time working or are laid off, then the employer may be required to pay guarantee payments, defined by statute as subject to a current maximum of £14.10 per day (reviewed annually by the Secretary of State) and limited to a maximum of five days in each three month period. There are several qualifying conditions:

- the employee must have been continuously employed for at least one month before the first guarantee payment is due

- employees on fixed-term contracts of three months or less will not qualify, unless previous service of more than three months has already been acquired

- no work must be done on the days claimed for guarantee payments (a day is defined as 24 hours from midnight to midnight).

Even if these conditions are met, there are circumstances in which eligibility for a guarantee payment will be lost:

- if the short-time working or lay-off is caused partly or wholly by a strike, lock-out or any other industrial action, involving either the employer or an associated employer, or

- if the employer has provided work that is *suitable in the circumstances*, and the employee refuses to perform the work. The work does not have to fall within the terms of the employee's contract, but must constitute a reasonable request in terms of the capabilities of the employee. For example, a coach trimmer was asked to work in the finishing department and refused. The tribunal decided the work was within his skills, although outside his contract, and therefore he was not entitled to a guarantee payment (*Purdy v Willowbrook International Ltd* 1977 IRLR 388)

- the employee must be available for work and comply with reasonable requirements aimed at ensuring availability. A decision to go home rather than wait for work to arrive, for example, can disqualify the employee from eligibility for a guarantee payment.

For information regarding the calculation of guarantee payments see Appendix 1.

Failure to Pay a Guarantee Payment

A tribunal will hear claims from employees that either they were eligible for guarantee pay and none has been paid, or that the full entitlement was not paid. Claims must be made within three months of the last workless day, although when this time limit is exceeded, the tribunal has discretion to hear the claim if it considers it was not reasonably practicable to submit the claim within the three months. If the claim is successful, the tribunal will order the employer to pay the monies due.

Entitlement to a Redundancy Payment

Once an employee has been on short-time working or laid off for:

- either four or more consecutive weeks, or
- a series of six or more weeks, of which no more than three were consecutive, in a period of 13 weeks

the employee can claim a redundancy payment.

The Procedure

- Once the above conditions have been met, the employee must give his or her employer written notice of intention to claim a redundancy payment within four weeks of the last week of lay-off or short-time working.

- If the employer does not wish to pay the redundancy payment, written counter notice must be given within seven days of the date the employee's notice was served. The employer must state that there is a reasonable expectation of returning to normal working, ie no short-time or lay-off within the next 4 weeks, for a period of not less than 13 weeks.
- The employee must resign, giving a week's notice or more if the contract requires it, to terminate the employment within the following time limits:

  (a) where no counter notice has been served by the employer:
    - within three weeks of the expiry of the seven day period
  (b) where counter notice is served, but then withdrawn:
    - within three weeks of the employer's service of the withdrawal notice
  (c) where counter notice has not been withdrawn:
    - within three weeks of the tribunal's decision.

Note: Weeks lost through strike or lock-out will not be taken into account when applying these redundancy pay provisions. Weeks lost due to *any other* form of industrial action do count. Further details are given in *Croner's Reference Book for Employers*.

3 Consultation with Trade Unions

Introduction

Quite apart from the requirement to consult with individuals affected by redundancy, UK law demands that employers consult collectively with their recognised trade unions. Failure to do this properly may bring heavy financial penalties.

Recognised Trade Unions

A recognised trade union is one that the employer recognises to any extent for collective bargaining. A union is recognised if it is an independent body, eg not an employer-sponsored staff association, and if one of the following two conditions applies:

- the company's recognition is set out clearly in a written agreement with the trade union, or
- the company negotiates with the trade union on such topics as pay rates, terms and conditions of employment, discipline or any other matters described by the **Trade Union and Labour Relations (Consolidation) Act 1992** (TULR(C)A) as matters for collective bargaining.

An employer must consult with an appropriate recognised trade union:

- if it represents people likely to be made redundant
- regardless of the number of people affected
- whether or not those people are members of that union
- whether or not the people wish to be so represented.

Wider Definition of Redundancy

For the purposes of consultation only, redundancy exists if someone is to be dismissed for a reason not related to that individual, or for a number of reasons all of which are not so related. Thus it will be necessary to meet the consultation requirements if, in order to change terms and conditions, you give notice of dismissal to your employees with a view to re-engaging them immediately on new terms.

The Consultation Process

Consultation means exchanging information and views in order to seek mutually acceptable solutions to problems affecting both parties. It is not enough for the employer merely to state his or her intentions.

The employer has a statutory duty to seek agreement with the trade union as soon as possible on ways to:

- avoid dismissing employees
- reduce the number of employees to be dismissed
- mitigate the consequences of the dismissals.

Failure to reach agreement does not prevent the employer from proceeding with the proposals, and by itself does not prove that he or she did not try. The employer should therefore take adequate time and care over consultation, and ensure that there is evidence that this was done.

For the purpose of consultation the employer must provide the recognised trade union with the following information:

- the reasons for the proposed redundancies
- the number and description of employees to be dismissed
- the total number of employees of each description at the establishment
- how employees are to be selected for redundancy
- the method proposed for carrying out the dismissals
- the period over which the dismissals are to take effect

- how any non-statutory redundancy payments are to be calculated.

Timing

Regardless of the number of employees involved, consultation must start as early as possible. The EC Collective Redundancies Directive 75/129 states that this is when redundancies are first *contemplated*.

If the employer proposes to dismiss between 10 and 99 employees at any one establishment within a 30 day period, consultation must begin at least 30 days before the first of these employees is dismissed. If the employer proposes to dismiss 100 or more employees at any one establishment within a 90 day period, consultation must begin at least 90 days before the first of these employees is dismissed.

As "contemplation" of redundancy is the point at which consultation should begin and, as the employer needs to provide the trade union with detailed proposals and information for that consultation, it is vital that the employer translates contemplation into firm proposals as quickly as possible.

Penalties

If the employer fails to meet these consultation requirements, a trade union may complain to the industrial tribunal. The employer's only defence is to prove to the tribunal's satisfaction that special circumstances made it not reasonably practicable to comply but that nevertheless all reasonably practicable steps towards compliance that circumstances allowed were taken.

It is not an acceptable defence to claim that a controlling employer — eg a distant owner or the overseas headquarters of a multinational group — prevented this or failed to provide appropriate information.

If the industrial tribunal upholds the trade union's complaint it will make a "protective award" to each employee affected of one week's pay for each week of the protective period. The length of the protective period will depend upon the tribunal's assessment of the seriousness of the employer's failure, but the award will be not greater than:

- 90 days' pay if 100 or more redundancies are involved within a 90 day period
- 30 days' pay if 10 or more redundancies are involved within a 30 day period
- 28 days' pay in any other case.

The employee loses his or her entitlement to a protective award if he or she unreasonably refuses renewals of the old contract or suitable alternative work.

This protective award may not be offset against other payments such as wages or pay in lieu of notice; conversely, wages or pay in lieu of notice may not be offset against the award.

Consulting with Non-unionised Employees

Under current UK statute law the employer is required to consult collectively only if the employees affected are represented by a recognised independent trade union. However, the European Directive on Collective Redundancies does not make this restriction — it requires consultation with "employee representatives". Therefore the European Commission is taking enforcement proceedings against the UK in the European Court of Justice. This means that:

- UK law probably will be brought into line with the Directive sometime in 1995, and
- meanwhile, an employee who has not been consulted as required by the Directive (ie is not represented by a recognised trade union) may make a direct appeal to the courts for his or her "European" rights.

In practice, therefore, an employer who is dealing with redundancy of employees not represented by a recognised trade union should nevertheless:

- consult with employee representatives in the same way and to the same time constraints as if they were representatives of a recognised trade union
- if there are fewer than 50 employees and no employee representatives, give the information about the redundancies to each individual affected.

Notifying the Department of Employment

Quite apart from the requirement to consult with trade unions, the employer must notify the Department of Employment if he or she proposes to dismiss 10 or more employees.

If 10 to 99 employees are to be dismissed from an establishment within a 30 day period, at least 30 days' prior notification must be given before the first person is dismissed.

If 100 or more employees are to be dismissed from an establishment within a 90 day period, at least 90 days' prior notification must be given before the first person is dismissed.

The information to be given is the same as that to be given to recognised trade unions, but in addition should include:

- the names of trade unions recognised by the employer as representing the employees affected
- the date consultation began with those trade unions.

The information should be submitted on Form HR1, available from local offices of the Department of Employment.

An employer who fails to meet the notification requirements may be fined up to £5000.

4   Defining Dismissal

Introduction

A dismissal on the grounds of redundancy involves consideration of a complicated mix of statutory and contractual entitlements. Employees will be entitled to notice, and this will be either the statutory minimum or the contractual, whichever is the greater. Notice may be worked or paid in lieu: if it is paid in lieu this needs to be taken into account when the redundancy payment is calculated. The right to a redundancy payment may be extinguished if the employee takes industrial action or refuses suitable alternative employment. If the employee accepts suitable alternative employment but is dismissed during the trial period, there may be a subsequent claim that this dismissal was unfair … and so on! All these possibilities will be discussed in the chapters that follow. The majority of redundant employees will have three distinct rights:

* the right to minimum notice
* the right to a redundancy payment
* the right to claim unfair dismissal.

All these rights depend on whether or not the circumstances of the employee's departure meet the various statutory requirements.

There are four main categories of dismissal for redundancy pay purposes:

* dismissal by the employer
* expiry of a fixed-term contract
* constructive dismissal
* failure to allow return from maternity leave.

Dismissal by the Employer

If the employer terminates the contract and the employee has one month's continuous service, then notice is due. However, if the employee has less than one month's continuous service then the employer might still be obliged to give contractual notice. The notice due will either be the statutory minimum entitlement or the notice entitlement due under the contract, whichever is the greater.

The statutory minimum is laid down by s.49 of the **Employment Protection (Consolidation) Act 1978**:

after 1 month's continuous service but less than 2 years'	1 week
after 2 years' continuous service	2 weeks

and then 1 extra week for each year of service, to a maximum of 12 weeks.

Notice does not have to be in writing, although it is advisable. It is important to distinguish between formal notice to terminate the contract and notice of impending redundancies. Various cases have illustrated that to warn of future redundancies does not constitute serving formal notice; employees who leave in these circumstances are deemed to have resigned and thereby lost their entitlement to redundancy pay (*Morton Sundour Fabrics Ltd v Shaw* (1966) ITR 84). Notice to end the contract must stipulate the day on which the contract will end.

Fixed-term Contract Expires

A fixed-term contract is a contract for a defined period of time, and s.55(2)(6) of the EP(C)A defines its expiry as a dismissal.

The expiry of a fixed-term contract may also entitle the employee in some circumstances to a redundancy payment. In *Lee v Notts County Council* (1980) IRLR 284, for example, a polytechnic lecturer's fixed-term contract expired and was not renewed. The Court of Appeal ruled that there had been a reduction in the requirement for lecturers and therefore he was dismissed and also entitled to a redundancy payment.

Section 142 of the EP(C)A includes provision for fixed-term contracts to be drafted to include waiver clauses excluding the right to claim unfair dismissal and/or a redundancy payment. A valid unfair dismissal waiver can be inserted in any contract for a period of one year or more and a redundancy payment waiver in fixed-term contracts of two years or more at any time before the contract expires. Fixed-term contracts are not invalidated by notice clauses, such as "one week's notice to be given by either party", and this will remove the potential for a breach of contract claim for the unexpired part of the contract, should it prove necessary to terminate the contract earlier than anticipated. To invoke the notice clause however will invalidate the waiver clause, ie if the employee has the necessary qualifying service then a claim of unfair dismissal and/or a redundancy payment becomes a possibility.

A suitable waiver clause is as follows.

It is a condition of this contract of employment that you agree to include, in the event of the expiry of the term of this employment without its being renewed or extended:

(a)   any right to a redundancy payment

(b)   any claim in respect of rights under s.54 of the **Employment Protection (Consolidation) Act 1978** *or any statutory modification or re-enactment thereof.*

If a fixed-term contract is too short to allow for the insertion of a valid waiver clause, and the employee has previously been employed, eg on a permanent basis or under previously temporary or fixed-term contracts, then on the expiry of the last fixed-term contract there may be a cumulative length of service of two years or more. This totalling of service under previous contracts is possible even when there have been gaps in employment. For more details on continuous service see Appendix 2.

In *Open University v Triesman* (1978) IRLR 114, a lecturer on a seven month fixed-term contract became entitled to claim unfair dismissal and redundancy payment as she had previously worked under an 18 month fixed-term contract and had accrued continuous employment exceeding two years. More recently however, the NI Court of Appeal in *Mulrine v University of Ulster* (1993) IRLR 547 has made a distinction between the extension or renewal of a fixed-term contract and re-engagement. In this case, the employee's two year fixed-term contract was extended by three months, two months before it was due to expire. The Court of Appeal ruled that as the work and terms and conditions of employment remained the same, the original contract had been extended, and therefore the waiver clause was valid. It would appear advisable, therefore, to stress in situations like these, that the original term has been extended, rather than a fresh contract issued.

The basis of a constructive dismissal is that the employer's conduct has caused the resignation. Lord Denning in *Western Excavating (ECC) Ltd v Sharp* (1978) IRLR 27, said *"An employee is entitled to treat himself as constructively dismissed if the employer is guilty of conduct which is a significant breach going to the root of the contract … or which shows that the employer no longer intends to be bound by one or more of the essential terms of the contract"*, and further explanation was also given: "sensible persons would have no difficulty in recognising conduct by an employer which brings the contract to an end". If a contractual term is breached, this can be either an express or an implied term.

Express Terms

The terms found in offer letters, handbooks and the written statement of terms of employment form the majority of the express terms of the contract, ie those terms expressly agreed by employer and employee.

Implied Terms

These terms arise from civil law, eg the duty on the employer to behave in a way that maintains mutual trust and confidence and to maintain a healthy working environment, as well as from statute, eg the **Equal Pay Act 1970**, and from custom and practice. The terms may not be found in writing, eg the right to a tea break or company transport, but the employer could be in breach of contract if the term is altered.

Constructive Dismissal

In redundancy situations, constructive dismissal claims can arise when:

- employees are relocated without their consent
- mobility clauses are invoked unreasonably, eg too little time to adjust/make preparations
- flexibility clauses are invoked unreasonably, eg the employee is not helped to adjust to duties not undertaken for some time
- employees are temporarily laid off without pay and there is no contractual provision for this.

The employee must leave in response to the breach if a claim of constructive dismissal is to succeed. If the employee continues to work under the changed conditions, then this can be interpreted as an agreement to accept the change in contract terms.

The employee must prove that he or she has been dismissed, ie the breach was sufficient to justify resignation, and which contractual term was breached. In *Gillies v Richard Daniels and Co Ltd* (1979) IRLR 457, Mr Gillies resigned when his pay was reduced by £1.50 per week. The EAT decided that there had been a breach of contract, but not significant enough to justify resignation, and therefore there was no dismissal. Constructive dismissal can be fair or unfair.

If a change of location is necessary in order, for example, to safeguard jobs, then an employee who resigns as a consequence may be able to establish constructive dismissal, but the employer may be able to demonstrate a fair reason for the reduction and reasonable behaviour in implementing it.

If the employee agrees to try out the new terms and conditions, then there is a period of time defined as the *common law trial period*. Working within this common law trial period is not regarded in law as an affirmation of the contract, which means that the employee can leave during the common law trial period and still claim constructive dismissal. The length of this trial period varies from case to case. Common law trial periods apply to any unilateral change of contract, including those that happen in redundancy situations, eg changes to place of work or the nature of the work.

The common law trial period exists under the old contract, as opposed to the statutory trial period which only applies when the old contract has come to an end and suitable alternative employment has been offered. If an employee is asked to try out an alternative job during the notice period this will constitute a common law trial period, and the right to a statutory trial period remains. It is advisable, therefore, in order to avoid confusion, to terminate the original contract, offer the alternative employment before it ends and issue a new contract within eight weeks of the start of the new employment.

Failure to Allow Return from Maternity Leave

A female employee who attempts to exercise her right to return and is refused because her job has been declared redundant is entitled to claim unfair dismissal and a redundancy payment. The employer must offer her any suitable alternative employment available, otherwise the dismissal will be automatically unfair, and must consider her for any alternatives that arise at any time during her maternity leave (*Philip Hodges & Co. v Kell* 1994 IRLR 569).

Dismissals that Qualify for Redundancy Payments

In addition to the dismissals above, there are other circumstances which can constitute dismissal for the purposes of entitlement to a redundancy payment. These are:

- resignation during notice
- dismissal by operation of law.

Employee's Resignation during Notice

Once the employer has served formal notice of dismissal for redundancy it is possible for employees to leave earlier, ie to resign, and still qualify for a redundancy payment. The employee may have alternative employment lined up or may want to concentrate on job-hunting. If there is mutual agreement to bring forward the termination date, there will still be a dismissal for redundancy pay purposes. If the employer does not wish the employee to leave early, then the employee must rely on certain statutory provisions regarding resignation under notice (s.85 of the EP(C)A). In order to retain entitlement to a redundancy payment, the employee's resignation must occur during the *obligatory period*.

The obligatory period is the period of notice the employer is required to give by statute, or by contract if that is longer. In redundancy situations, some employers give a longer notice period, eg because it is easier to administer one three month notice period for 20 employees than have 20 employees on varying lengths of notice. The shorter-serving employees will not be within the obligatory period when the three months' notice is given. The obligatory period is the period of notice which should have been given to expire on the date the longer notice ends. The start of the obligatory period therefore is found by counting backwards from the termination date.

If the employee resigns during the obligatory period, entitlement may still be lost if the employer issues a counter notice. Section 85(3) of the EP(C)A allows an employer to withhold a redundancy payment if the following steps are followed:

- the employer issues a written notice before the expiry of the employee's notice

- the notice states that:

  - the employee is required to withdraw his or her notice, and to continue to work until the end of the employer's original notice

  - unless the employee complies, the employer will contest any liability to pay a redundancy payment.

Defining the obligatory periods

All 3 employees given 12 weeks' notice

	Notice entitlement	Obligatory period
Employee A: 3 years' service	Statutory minimum, ie 3 weeks	Begins after 9 weeks of notice completed
Employee B: 2 years' service	1 month's contractual notice	Begins after 8 weeks (more or less depending on how the *calendar* months fall)
Employee C: 14 years' service	Statutory minimum, ie 12 weeks	Begins at same time as formal notice

---

If this procedure is not followed exactly, the employee will still be entitled to a redundancy payment. In any event an industrial tribunal will hear claims from employees whose redundancy payments have been withheld and, after considering the reasons of both parties for their actions, will decide what amount, if any, should be awarded.

Dismissal by Operation of Law

This is defined as the termination of the contract by an event which makes future performance impossible or radically different. The "event" must rest solely with the employer — the imprisonment or ill-health of the employee would not fall within this definition.

Events falling within this category include:

- death or retirement of the employer
- appointment of a receiver by the court
- complete destruction of the business premises.

Terminations of Contracts that do not Qualify for Redundancy Payments

These are as follows:

- transfer of business ownership
- mutual agreement
- completion of apprenticeships
- renewal or re-engagement.

Transfer of Business Ownership

In common law, a transfer of business ownership would terminate the contracts of the employees in that business and they would become eligible for a redundancy payment. This can be overridden, however, if the transfer falls within the scope of the **Transfer of Undertakings Regulations 1981** (SI 1981 No. 1794). If these regulations apply, then the employment contracts of those staff employed by the vendor immediately before the transfer will automatically become contracts with the purchaser, even if several transactions are involved, and continuity of employment is preserved. The new employer assumes the majority of the duties and obligations of the previous employer. An employee who objects to being transferred will be exempt from the regulations and the transfer will terminate the contract. The employee will be eligible to claim redress against the transferee — if, for example, an unsuitable offer of alternative work was made, there is the possibility of a claim of constructive dismissal and a redundancy payment.

There are several aspects to consider as follows.

The nature of the business

As a result of amendments introduced by the **Trade Union Reform and Employment Rights Act 1993** (TURERA), commercial and non-commercial undertakings fall within the regulations. The business or activity must transfer as an economic entity and a going concern; a transfer of assets or a share takeover would not meet the requirements. A company who took over the premises and machinery at a suit factory, for example, and intended to make different quality suits by a different production method was deemed to be carrying on a different basis, and therefore the transfer was not within the regulations (*Melon v Hector Powe Ltd* (1980) IRLR 479).

The nature of the transfer

If the activity, or part of it, is being disposed of, relevant transfers can be by:

- sale of the business
- a merger between companies
- the integration of a subsidiary
- transfers of a licence or franchise
- inheritance.

Transfer of property does not need to be a factor; it can be a transfer of funding and clients — *Dr Sophie Redmond Stichting v Bartol and ors* (1992) IRLR 366.

Effect of transfer on employment contracts

Employees with the necessary qualifying service who transfer and find their contracts changed unilaterally, ie without their consent, can resign and claim constructive dismissal and a redundancy payment. If employees are dismissed before or after a transfer the dismissal will be automatically unfair if the reason (or principal reason) is the transfer or a reason connected with it. The only exception to this is where the dismissal was due to an economic, technical or organisational reason entailing changes in the workforce. Where this reason is established it must then be demonstrated that the employer acted reasonably in treating this as a sufficient reason for dismissal. Redundancy, for example, could well be an economic, technical or organisational reason, but the employer would still have to show that there had been fair selection, adequate consultation and a search for suitable alternative employment. If the redundancies are by the purchaser, the "old" procedure for selection will have transferred over with the employees and therefore there is a risk of unfair dismissal if they are selected in breach of it.

These provisions have given rise to questions over whether employees are protected if they were not still employed at the moment of transfer, ie "immediately before" the transfer took place. In *Secretary of State for Employment v Spence and Others* (1986) IRLR 248, the Court of Appeal ruled that employees dismissed by the receiver three hours prior to the sale (and subsequently re-employed by the new owners the following day) were not employed "immediately before" the transfer and were therefore entitled to redundancy payments.

This view has been modified, however, by the decision of the House of Lords in *Litster and Ors v Forth Dry Dock and*

Engineering Co Ltd (1989) IRLR 161. If the dismissal is for economic, technical or organisational reasons, then the *Spence* interpretation applies and liability for the dismissals remains with the transferor. If the dismissal is not by virtue of economic, technical or organisational reasons, then "immediately before" is to be construed as "would have been employed immediately before if he or she had not been unfairly dismissed", ie the transferee becomes liable.

The Employment Appeal Tribunal (EAT) has recently confirmed this approach in *UK Security Services (Midlands) Ltd v Gibbons and Others* EAT 104/90. Receivers sold the business to UK Security Services and the employees were dismissed three hours prior to the sale. As their employer was insolvent, the employees applied for redundancy payments from the National Insurance Fund (see Appendix 5). This application was refused on the basis that there had been a transfer of an undertaking, and UK Security Services were therefore obliged to make the payments. On appeal, the EAT confirmed that the dismissals were intended to secure a better price for the business, which was not an economic, technical or organisational reason, and therefore UK Security Services were required to make the redundancy payments.

Mutual Agreement

When the employer and employee enter into an agreement to terminate, normally involving a financial settlement, this termination does not constitute dismissal. The issue can prove difficult to define in cases of voluntary redundancy and voluntary early retirement. When employees opt for early retirement, without any pressure being applied to do so, then the termination is likely to be seen as by mutual consent (*Birch and Humber v University of Liverpool* (1985) IRLR 165).

If employees are offered and accept voluntary early retirement whilst under notice of redundancy, they will not be entitled to redundancy payments, as this is viewed as a mutual agreement to terminate, not dismissal (*Scott and others v Coalite Fuels and Chemicals Ltd* (1988) IRLR 131).

If, however, the employer has asked for volunteers because redundancies are inevitable, then the employees have volunteered to be selected and must await the employer's decision as to who will be dismissed. In these circumstances the volunteers will be regarded as dismissed on the grounds of redundancy.

Completion of Apprenticeships

The EP(C)A defines dismissal on the expiry of a fixed-term contract as only occurring when there is "no renewal under the same contract". An apprenticeship can only be served once and, therefore, as there is no possibility of renewal under the same contract, there is no dismissal — and no redundancy payment.

Renewal or Re-engagement

If a redundant employee accepts an offer of renewal of the existing contract or re-engagement under a new contract before the original employment ends, and the renewal or re-engagement is to take effect immediately or not more than four weeks after the ending of the employment under the old contract, then the original dismissal is overridden and there is no right to a redundancy payment. If however the employee refuses the offer or decides during the statutory trial period that the job is not acceptable, the right to receive a redundancy payment will depend on the suitability of the offer and the reasonableness of the employee in turning it down. This must be decided by the employer in the first instance, and subsequently by a tribunal if the payment is withheld. Further details are given in Chapter 9 on Redundancy Pay.

Common Questions

Q. We moved premises four weeks ago and all our staff agreed to the move. Our contracts all gave the place of work as the old location, which is several miles away. One of our receptionists has now resigned and is claiming constructive dismissal and a redundancy payment. Does she have a basis for this?

A. *It depends whether or not you can argue that she expressly agreed to the change in location, eg in writing or in discussion with her manager. If so, then there was a mutual agreement to the change of terms. If this was not the case (eg if she expressed reservations, but said she would give it a try) then arguably she has worked on under a common law trial period and has now terminated the old contract by resigning. She would, therefore, have the basis for both claims. Consider, however, that her contract may have contained an implied mobility clause (see Chapter 5) and, alternatively, that this was a fair constructive dismissal, eg did you behave reasonably in terms of consultation and considering alternatives to the new location?*

Q. We have issued formal redundancy notices to dismiss staff at one of our depots and the notice is due to expire next week. Unfortunately, the staff at another depot are now on strike and we need to transfer the work over to finish the order in time. The staff however are refusing to work on beyond the end of next week. Can we withhold their redundancy pay?

A. *Notice once given cannot be unilaterally withdrawn. It would be as well, therefore, to regard this as an offer of alternative employment. If the work is different from the work performed under the present contract then the staff are entitled to a four week trial period. If the employees still refuse to work on, redundancy payments can be withheld on the basis that an offer of suitable alternative employment has been unreasonably refused. (This is discussed in more detail in Chapter 9.)*

5 Defining Redundancy

Introduction

Redundancy is one of the five potentially fair reasons for dismissal, set out in s.57 of the **Employment Protection (Consolidation) Act 1978** (EP(C)A). The reasons are:

- capability or qualifications of the employee for performing work of the kind he or she was employed to do
- the employee's conduct
- the employee was redundant
- that continued employment would have been breaking the law
- there was some other substantial reason that justified dismissal.

When a claim of unfair dismissal on the grounds of redundancy has been made, the employer must show that the reason, ie redundancy, falls within the statutory definition of redundancy given in s.81 of the EP(C)A. If it does not, then the employer has failed to prove the reason and the dismissal will be unfair. This is irrespective of a genuine belief on the employer's part that the employees were redundant. Employers are often advised, if there is any doubt about meeting the statutory definition, to plead in the alternative — normally "redundancy, or some other substantial reason".

The statutory definition must also be met for entitlement to a redundancy payment, but the tribunal is required to presume entitlement under s.91 of the EP(C)A. This means that an employer who wishes to contest it must show that the reason for the dismissal does *not* meet the definition of redundancy. This difference in the burden of proof between the two claims can give rise to some curious results at tribunal!

Employees can raise claims for unfair dismissal irrespective of whether a redundancy payment was made, and claim a redundancy payment and not unfair dismissal, and claim both unfair dismissal and a redundancy payment — all are possible, as long as the qualifying conditions are met (see Appendix 3 and Chapter 7).

The statutory definition in s.81(2) paragraphs (a) and (b) is:

"… an employee who is dismissed is taken to be dismissed by reason of redundancy if the dismissal is wholly or mainly attributable to:

(a) the fact that the employer has ceased, or intends to cease, to carry on the business for the purposes of which the employee was employed by him, or has ceased or intends to cease to carry on that business in the place where the employee was so employed, or

(b) the fact that the requirements of that business for employees to carry out work of a particular kind or for employees to carry out work of a particular kind in the place where they were so employed, have ceased or diminished or are expected to cease or diminish."

Various aspects of this can be examined in turn: *"wholly or mainly"*.

The dismissal must be caused predominantly by reason of redundancy, eg if an employee is under-performing, then the tribunal may decide that redundancy was a mutually acceptable way of describing the employee's departure, and that the dismissal was actually for incapability, rather than redundancy. Changes to terms and conditions, eg changes in shift patterns, may result in dismissals of those employees who cannot comply, but these dismissals will probably be for "some other substantial reason", rather than redundancy.

The Closure of the Business

The employer may cease carrying out the business on a *permanent or temporary* basis, as both fall within the definition. If the business is closed for anything over four weeks then the employees may become entitled to a redundancy payment and may also sue for breach of contract if they are laid off in breach of contract (see Chapter 2 on Lay-off). Moving residents from a nursing home into hospital accommodation whilst the home is refurbished could therefore result in redundancy dismissals of the carers in the home if their services are not needed and the home cannot afford to lay them off with pay.

If one employer has ceased trading altogether, but has sold the business as a going concern, then the transfer could fall within the **Transfer of Undertakings Regulations 1981** and the employees will not be redundant (see Chapter 4).

The Nature of the Business

"The business" has a wider definition than pure commercial activity, and effectively means any commercial or non profit-making activity. A charity, for example a hospital, and a social club would both fall within the definition, as would any trade or profession.

An employer may run more than one business and each business can be considered autonomous in terms of the statutory definition. If, for example, an employer runs a restaurant in town and also runs a factory plus canteen, there is no obligation to look for alternative work for the restaurant staff within the factory.

Associated Employers

If an employer is a limited company and has control, or is controlled by, another company or if both companies are controlled by a third, then the businesses are "associated employers". For the purposes of the statutory redundancy provisions, the businesses can be aggregated, unless it is possible to establish that redundancy has occurred without including the other businesses. This has two implications: first, if employer A has an expanding business, and the business of associated company B is contracting, the dismissals of the company B employees will still be for redundancy. Second, if company B employees are given jobs in company A, and company A employees are dismissed, then their dismissals may well be for redundancy. This is known as "bumping" and is discussed further in Chapter 7.

"In the Place of Work"

The place of work is now defined by case law as the location(s) the employee can be required to work under the terms of the contract, rather than the place of work when notice is given. Contracts that narrowly define the place of work, eg to one site or one office rather than "any of our locations" or "anywhere within the UK", give employers less opportunity for transfers within the terms of the contract. If work was available at another site and the contract did not allow for a transfer within the definition of "place of work", then the employee would have to be dismissed on the grounds of redundancy and offered re-employment at the new site. Employers have adopted the use of mobility clauses in contracts to give greater flexibility in changing the place of work thereby avoiding dismissals. In *Rank Xerox Ltd v Churchill and others* (1988) IRLR 280 the company moved from London to Marlow and six secretaries resigned, claiming constructive dismissal and redundancy payments. Their contracts included the clause "the company may require you to transfer to another location". The tribunal ruled that this clause was too vague to have any effect, that a proviso of locations within a reasonable daily travelling distance should have been included and that Marlow was not within that distance. The employer appealed and the EAT overturned the tribunal's decision. In the EAT's opinion, the industrial tribunal had erred in applying the test of reasonableness to a straightforward express term. The express term was acceptable, and therefore the secretaries had no right to a redundancy payment as their place of work still existed — in Marlow.

The mobility clause may even be implied — in *Jones v Association Tunnelling Co Ltd* (1981) IRLR 477 the EAT commented that there was an implied mobility clause that defined the place of work as anywhere within reasonable daily reach of home. Any mobility clause however, express or implied, must still be implemented reasonably, eg with adequate consultation and warning, or the employee may resign and have grounds to claim constructive dismissal.

These cases had provided definitive guidance to those drafting contract terms, but some doubt as to their effectiveness has been raised recently by the EAT's decision in *Bass Leisure Ltd v Thomas* (1994) IRLR 8. The contract in question contained a mobility clause stating that the company reserved the right to transfer employees to suitable alternative places of work. The EAT commented that "place of work" in s.81(2)(a) of the EP(C)A was intended to be one, unique place, and that whereas a contractual term defining the place of work could be wide enough to cover several locations, to rely on a mobility clause which was only a term giving the employer the right to vary the place of work was outside the s.81(2) provisions. In the EAT's opinion, mobility clauses are relevant to constructive dismissal claims, but should not be taken into account in defining the place of work in redundancy cases. Until further case law is established, it would appear that employers are best advised when completing the written statement to consider carefully the description of the place of work and to rely on this, rather than the mobility clause in redundancy situations. The TURERA provisions on written statements do now require place of work to be included in the written statement, whereas prior to 30 November 1993 this was not the case.

Requirements for Work of a Particular Kind

The critical element in this definition is the requirement for employees to do work *of a particular kind*. An obvious example would be a factory dismissing operatives because orders have reduced substantially. The factory could dismiss some operatives because their section has been mechanised and output has remained constant, or even because reorganisation of the work has led to greater efficiency and the need for fewer operatives. These dismissals are commonly recognised as redundancy dismissals. It is possible, however, for the number of employees on the payroll to remain constant, or even increase, and yet some employees be dismissed as redundant. This is because of the interpretations of "work of a particular kind" — see page 52.

There are principally three possibilities:

- the requirements diminish because the business diminishes
- the requirements diminish because the work is computerised/mechanised
- the requirements diminish because the work is done in another way.

The requirements diminish because the business diminishes

There may be a drop in demand, for example, or a gap between orders. This type of redundancy is quite often easy to define because of the clear link between the drop in business activity and the overstaffing that it causes. Dismissal on these grounds may be preceded by lay-offs or short-time working.

The requirements diminish because the work is computerised/mechanised

In this context, the volume of work could have increased, but because of the change in work method fewer employees are needed to carry it out. The advent of new technology, eg introducing robots, computers and electronic surveillance, has led to increasing numbers of redundancies on these grounds.

The requirements diminish because the work is done in another way

This definition is less easily identifiable and the one most likely to feature as "redundancy *or* some other substantial reason". The overall number of employees may remain the same, the amount of work may remain the same, new jobs may be created, and yet there can still be grounds for redundancy. The decisive factor is what has happened to work "of a particular kind". The following cases illustrate how this phrase has been interpreted.

- **The work may be given to outside contractors.** In *Bromby and Hoare v Evans* (1972) ICR 113 two employees were found to be fairly dismissed as redundant when their work was given to two self-employed labourers. The business was expanding and their work still existed, but the requirement for *them* had diminished.

- **The work may be given to other employees.** The manager may take over the subordinate's duties, eg as in *Carry All Motors Law v Pennington* (1980) IRLR 455, or the work may be redistributed and covered by overtime, eg *Delanair Ltd v Mead* (1976) IRLR 340.

  The EAT however was not willing to apply this definition in *Frame It v Brown* 1993 EAT (177/93). One job was distributed amongst three others, and the employers sought to rely on *Carry All Motors*, and lost at tribunal and EAT. In the EAT's view, if reallocation of duties could constitute redundancy, employers would be less keen to reorganise and therefore business efficiency would be impaired. Employers will need to proceed with caution until future decisions clarify the case law on this point. It would certainly appear advisable to plead "some other substantial reason" as an alternative to redundancy, in case the first reason fails.

- **The work may be upgraded.** One manager may be appointed to do a more high powered job in place of two redundant employees, as in *Robinson v British Island Airways Ltd* (1977) IRLR 477, or the new machinery may require a better skilled operator, eg *Denton v Neepsend Ltd* (1976) IRLR 164.

- **The type of employee required may change.** In *Murphy v Epsom College* (1985) ICR 80, a plumber who could do some engineering work was replaced by an engineer who could undertake plumbing, and the Court of Appeal ruled that Mr Murphy was dismissed as redundant.

- **Re-organising leads to a change of duties.** In *MacFisheries Ltd v Findlay and Others* (1985) ICR 160 employees dismissed for refusing to change to day shifts successfully claimed redundancy payments, because the work done on the day shift was *different* work.

Note: A change in hours is not in itself a change in work of a particular kind; see *Johnson and Dutton v Notts Combined Police Authority* on page 54.

What is "Work of a Particular Kind?"

The answer to this question is determined by the duties the employee can be required to do within the contract of employment, as a result of the Court of Appeal's decision in *Nelson v BBC* (1977) IRLR 148. Mr Nelson was employed as a producer on the Caribbean service and dismissed as redundant when the service closed down and he refused alternative work. The Court of Appeal ruled that as Mr Nelson's contract stated that he could be required to work in any department and the work existed, he was not dismissed on the grounds of redundancy and therefore had been unfairly dismissed.

This decision illustrated that it is the duties as defined by the contract, rather than the work performed at the time, which constitutes "work of a particular kind". The wider the contractual definition of work, the greater the likelihood that employees can be transferred to different jobs within the terms of the original contract, rather than be made redundant and offered re-employment. The Court of Appeal's ruling was re-confirmed as guidance by the EAT in *Pink v I White and Z White and Co (Earls Barton) Ltd* (1985) IRLR 489. An employee whose contract described him as a "making and finishing room operative" was dismissed from his job as a "pre-sole fitter" and replaced by another employee. He claimed this was not within the statutory definition of redundancy and therefore it was an unfair dismissal. The industrial tribunal and the EAT ruled that the overall requirement for "making and finishing room operatives" had diminished, and therefore he was redundant and fairly dismissed.

Unfair Redundancy — Unsound Reasons

The employer must demonstrate that the definition is met, but does not have to justify the reason why the redundancies arose — they may have resulted from poor management of the business or perhaps a downturn in orders could have been avoided, but the tribunal cannot take these factors into account.

Once the tribunal has heard the employer's explanation, it will make a decision on whether or not the dismissal is by virtue of redundancy. The following cases illustrate how this approach works in practice.

• **Capability dismissal found to be for redundancy** — *Marshall v Harland and Wolff Ltd and another* (1972) IRLR 90

  Mr Marshall had been off sick for 18 months, when the decision was taken to close the workshop in which he worked. The employer claimed he was dismissed because of his sickness and refused him a redundancy payment. The National Industrial Relations Court (NIRC) awarded a payment on the basis that his employer had not taken any steps to dismiss him prior to the closure, and therefore in the NIRC's view he had been dismissed for redundancy.

- **Industrial action may cause redundancies** — *Sanders and others v Ernest A Neale Ltd (1974) IRLR 236*

  Employees refused to work overtime or take on the work of redundant colleagues and were dismissed. Eventually the factory was closed due to the dispute, and the remaining employees were given redundancy payments. The NIRC held that the first dismissals were due to industrial action, not redundancy.

- **A withdrawal of funding** — *Association of University Teachers v University of Newcastle (1988) IRLR 10*

  A lecturer's fixed-term contract was not renewed because funding had run out. The tribunal decided that the reason for the dismissal was lack of funds, not redundancy. The EAT held that the tribunal had erred in looking at the reason *why* there was no longer a requirement for a lecturer; it was the *fact* of the redundancy that was important. The dismissal did fall within the statutory definition — there was a continuing need for teaching, but due to no funding the requirement ceased.

- **Problem employees declared redundant** — *Maund v Penrith District Council (1984) IRLR 24*

  A trade union activist created enough problems with his employer to prompt them to dismiss him, and his department, as redundant. The EAT ruled that this action was a contrivance to remove him from the workplace, and that the dismissal was for trade union activities, not redundancy.

- **Changes in working hours** — *Johnson and Dutton v Notts Combined Police Authority (1974) IRLR 20*

  Two clerks were asked to change from fixed hours to a shift system; they refused and were subsequently dismissed. Their claim for redundancy payments failed because there had been no change to the nature of the

work or the number of employees required to do it.
Dismissal was for "some other substantial reason".

- **Employer attempts to save money** — *Hartwell Commercial group Ltd v Brand and Jones* EAT 506/92

  Two senior managers were covered by a covenant binding all future owners of the business to pay very generous redundancy payments if they ever became redundant. Two take-overs later, they were both dismissed for insubordination and poor performance. The industrial tribunal and the EAT both found that the principal reason for the dismissal was redundancy — the managers had been dismissed as part of a cost saving exercise and, although there was some evidence of poor performance, this reason had been chosen primarily to avoid the cost of the enhanced redundancy payments.

Next Step…

Once the tribunal is satisfied that there has been a dismissal, and that this dismissal is for a reason that falls within the statutory definition, the next question to be addressed is "was it a fair selection…?".

6 Establishing Fair Selection

Introduction

In situations where the employer has dismissed either all employees or just one employee who occupies a unique position, the question of unfair selection does not arise. Employees who cannot claim unfair selection can still claim that the reason for their dismissal does not fit within the statutory definition of redundancy given in s.81 of the **Employment Protection (Consolidation) Act 1978** (EP(C)A) and/or that the employer acted unreasonably within the terms of s.57(3) of the EP(C)A (see Chapter 7).

When some employees are dismissed and others retained, the redundant employees can challenge the method of selection. If any aspect of their selection is found to fall short of the legal requirements, the dismissal will be unfair. The legal provisions are given in s.59 of the EP(C)A.

Section 59 states:

"where ... it is shown that the circumstances ... applied equally to one or more employees in the same undertaking who held positions similar to him who have not been dismissed, and either the reason ... for which the employee was selected was an inadmissible one, or he was selected for dismissal in contravention of a customary arrangement or agreed procedure ... and there was no special reason justifying a departure from that arrangement or procedure ... the dismissal shall be regarded as unfair."

What is an Undertaking?

This question will arise whenever employees are based at different locations. The issue is essentially one for the tribunal to decide on the facts put before them — there is no legal definition. If the employer can demonstrate that there is an agreement in existence that defines the undertaking, the tribunal will take note of this. Tribunals have tended to take a fairly wide interpretation and have taken note of accounting procedures, purchasing arrangements and insurance cover. In one case for example two factories with one factory manager, one bonus scheme and movement of labour between them were considered to constitute one undertaking. Too narrow a definition could suggest the employer is attempting to manipulate the selection criteria — the implications need to be considered carefully.

Who are Employees in Similar Positions?

The answer to this question determines which employees should be included in the pool of selection (see page 64). Factors to be taken into account include common skills, qualifications, similar work and any flexibility between jobs. The full range of duties should be considered, not just those undertaken at the time of selection. For example, five employees were made redundant from an assembly department, including one who had recently transferred from the packing department; there were shorter serving employees (ie new recruits) in the packing department and the tribunal ruled that these employees were "employees in similar positions" who should have been included in the pool of selection (*Thomas and Betts Manufacturing Co Ltd v Harding* (1978) IRLR 213).

What are the Inadmissible Reasons?

These are reasons that render the dismissal automatically unfair. The range of inadmissible reasons has been increased as a result of TURERA and is now:

- selection due to the employee's actions in taking steps to promote health and safety standards in the workplace.

  Section 57A(1), EP(C)A

- selection for asserting a statutory right

  Section 60A(1), EP(C)A

- selection on the grounds of pregnancy or maternity

  Section 60, EP(C)A

Note: currently, dismissal on these grounds would be raised as unlawful sex discrimination by those employees with less than two years' service, and those employees with qualifying service who claim under s.60 are covered by "old" s.60 — see page 61.

Trade Union Grounds

In addition to the inadmissible reasons, s.153 of TULR(C)A states that if the employee is selected on trade union grounds, the dismissal will be automatically unfair. Section 152(1) defines these grounds as selection because of membership or activities connected with an independent trade union, or non-membership of a trade union.

These four reasons are discussed below in more detail.

Health and safety

If the employee is a safety representative, appointed by either the employer or fellow employees, and is selected for redundancy as a result of the role he or she performs, then the dismissal will be unfair; no qualifying service is necessary and the bar on applicants over normal retirement age will not apply.

Any employee who has:

- raised health and safety issues directly with management because there was no representative
- left or intended to leave the workplace because of perceived risks
- refused to return, *or*

- taken steps to protect personal safety and the safety of others, *and* considers that this has led to unfair selection,

may also appeal to the tribunal on these grounds.

The employee can apply for interim relief (see Appendix 4) and receive a special award (see Chapter 7).

Assertion of a statutory right

The statutory rights in question are mainly those that do not require two years' qualifying service and the intention of this provision, introduced into the EP(C)A by TURERA, is to protect those employees without the qualifying service to claim unfair dismissal, if they are dismissed whilst asserting a "statutory right".

Asserting the right means bringing proceedings against the employer, eg by complaining to an industrial tribunal OR making an allegation to the employer or any other party that the right has been infringed. The employee does not need to have qualified for the right(s) in question, and neither does the right have to have been infringed (as long as the allegation was made in good faith).

There is no upper age limit for these claims.

These statutory rights are:

- all rights conferred under the EP(C)A — which includes the right to guarantee payments, and to look for work
- rights under the **Wages Act 1986** — eg unlawful deductions from pay
- the right to minimum notice
- rights under the TULR(C)A, eg time off for union duties and activities.

Selection due to pregnancy or maternity

Section 60 of the EP(C)A has been amended by TURERA.

TURERA contains a range of provisions to protect the employment of female employees who are pregnant or who have recently given birth. Under the terms of the Pregnant

Workers Directive, these provisions must have been enacted by 19 October 1994.

The old s.60 of the EP(C)A provided certain exceptions to the rule that all dismissals linked to pregnancy, or any other reason connected with pregnancy, will be automatically unfair. For example, if the employee is incapable of carrying out her duties due to the pregnancy *or* is barred by statute (eg the **Ionising Radiations Regulations 1985**) *and* the employer acted reasonably, the dismissal can be fair.

Under the "new" s.60, these exceptions have disappeared.

The dismissal will be automatically unfair if the reason or principal reason for the dismissal is:

(a) pregnancy or any other reason connected with pregnancy

(b) childbirth or any reason connected with it, where the 14 week maternity leave period is ended by the dismissal

(c) that the employee took or availed herself of the benefits of the basic 14 week period and is dismissed when the basic leave period expires

(d) childbirth or any reason connected with it, where the contract is terminated within four weeks of the end of basic leave, and the employee is absent due to medical reasons, which were certified by a medical practitioner, before the end of the basic leave period

(e) that the employee was suspended because of health and safety restrictions linked to the pregnancy or maternity.

No qualifying service is needed for (a)–(e) above.

If the reason for the dismissal is *redundancy*, under "new" s.60, but a suitable alternative job exists and the employer fails to offer it, the dismissal will be automatically unfair. No qualifying service is needed. If no alternative exists or the employee rejects the job offered, then the employment can be terminated by reason of redundancy and the employee will be eligible to claim unfair dismissal and a redundancy payment, as long as she has the necessary qualifying service.

TURERA and redundancy of pregnant employees: genuine redundancies, where the pregnant employee was selected on objective criteria which were applied fairly, and where she has been treated reasonably, will still qualify as fair dismissal. The employer must proceed carefully however and check for discriminatory practices as well as any breaches of the TURERA provisions. Employees will be able to raise separate claims of unfair dismissal and discrimination and the limit on compensation for sex discrimination has now been abolished (see Chapter 7).

Trade union membership and activities
This is selection on the grounds that the employee:

- was, or proposed to become, a member of an independent trade union
- had taken part, or proposed to take part, in the activities of an independent trade union at *an appropriate time,* ie at a time within working hours, approved by the employer
- was not a member of any trade union or a particular trade union, or of one of a number of particular trade unions or had refused or proposed to refuse to become or remain a member.

The first two provisions relate only to independent trade unions, but dismissal for non-membership applies to both independent and non-independent unions. (See Glossary for definition of an independent trade union.) Selection on these grounds will enable the employee to apply for interim relief (see Appendix 4) and to receive a special award (see Chapter 7).

Breaches of a Customary Arrangement or Agreed Procedure, with no Special Reasons (section 59(1)(b) EP(C)A)

What is a customary arrangement and an agreed procedure?
There is no statutory definition for either of these, and their exact nature and the distinctions between them, have evolved through case law.

- In *Thomas and Betts v Harding* (see page 58) the EAT said that an *agreed procedure* is one *expressly* agreed between employer and employees or their representatives. The agreement did not have to be in writing, but the procedure agreed should operate fairly between different categories and classes of employee.

- If the union has not previously objected to certain selection criteria, then this can be taken as evidence of an *implied procedure* (*Henry v Ellerman City Liners Ltd* (1984) IRLR 409).

- An *agreed procedure* has contractual overtones, whilst a *customary arrangement* is merely a question of what tends to happen in practice, irrespective of whether or not it is agreed (*Suflex Ltd v Thomas and Others* (1978) IRLR 435).

A customary agreement must have "the binding force and the clarity which would be expected in an expressly agreed procedure" (*Tayside Health Board v Doogan* EAT 226/93).

There seems, unfortunately, to be little clear distinction between the two. A procedure must be *agreed*, but an arrangement that the union has not objected to will be an implied procedure, according to *Henry v Ellerman City Liners Ltd*.

Employers are probably best advised to agree, whenever possible, the content of the selection procedure clearly, in advance and in writing, in an attempt to avoid disputes over interpretation at the time when redundancies are made, or subsequently.

The special reasons

Any departure from the procedure or arrangement may mean that the employer has to demonstrate at tribunal that the departure was justified, eg in terms of the needs of the business, and also that the new method was still fair, objective and valid. The "old" procedure is often last in first out (LIFO). Employers who wish to abandon the LIFO procedure, or incorporate other criteria as well, must be able to demonstrate that they attempted to negotiate these changes with employees and their representatives.

Note: Claims under s.59(1)(b) require the applicant to be under the age limit and have the necessary qualifying service.

Unreasonable selection

The employer's behaviour in implementing the procedure or arrangement will be assessed at tribunal by the general test of fairness applied to all dismissals in s.57(3) of the EP(C)A "… whether in the circumstances … the employer acted reasonably or unreasonably …". In the context of unfair aspects of selection, there are three main areas for consideration:

- the pool of selection
- selection criteria
- consultation.

The pool of selection

The choice of an incorrect pool will render the dismissal unfair. Various cases (*Cowen v Haden Carrier Ltd* (1982) IRLR 255 and *Pink v I White and Z White and Co (Earls Barton) Ltd* (1985) IRLR 489) suggest that the pool should include all those whose contracts include the work now diminishing. If only one particular function, trade or skill group is affected, assessing the nature of the pool can be quite straightforward. If there is some degree of flexibility between jobs, however, it is as well to take the contractual description into account. Those employers who have favoured wide-ranging job titles or job descriptions (eg to aid job flexibility and avoid redundancies) will find determining the pool more problematic than those whose contracts have been more specific, eg "factory operative" v "finisher" or "trimmer" or "clerical assistant" v "wages clerk".

The employer must be able to demonstrate the rationale behind the unit selected, and also show that efforts were made to agree this unit with employees and their representatives.

Selection Criteria

The EAT's guidance in *Williams and Ors v Compair Maxam Ltd* (1982) IRLR 83 is still valid:

> *"the employer will seek to establish criteria for selection which so far as possible do not depend solely upon the opinion of the person making the selection but can be objectively checked against such things as attendance record, efficiency at the job, experience, or length of service".*

Any selected employee must be consulted, and be able to have free access to any information that was utilised in selecting that employee. See page 71 for a model redundancy selection assessment form.

Criteria must be applied fairly and consistently so that each individual selected has been identified by the same method of assessment.

Subjective judgments can form part of the assessment, as long as it can be demonstrated that there was a fair and balanced approach, eg the criteria were reasonable and appropriate, and not designed to select employees who had become unpopular.

The ACAS *Guidance Booklet to Redundancy Handling* suggests that selection based on skills or qualifications will help retain a balanced workforce for the future, and discusses the pros and cons of LIFO and other criteria.

Employers have adopted a wide range of criteria and some of these are given below.

LIFO — Last In, First Out

Basically those with the shortest continuous service are dismissed first. This method has a long history, is widespread and is often favoured by unions and employers. LIFO is easy to use and understood by all involved, and is less costly than dismissing the longer-serving employees. Employers are finding however that LIFO can mean the remaining workforce does not have the skills, experience and versatility necessary for future success. The EAT's view appears to be that it is unreasonable to ignore LIFO altogether, although it does not have to take precedence over other factors such as job performance and skills (*B L Cars Ltd v Lewis* (1983) IRLR 58). This view was confirmed again more recently in *Brook v London Borough of Haringey* (1992) IRLR 478, when the EAT commented that "employers, trade unions, ACAS and indeed, commonsense, all recognise that length of service is an essential ingredient in any redundancy selections save in the most exceptional circumstances".

The employer must be clear how continuous service will be assessed and must apply the rules consistently, for example:

- will service be assessed as in the job, in the section or within the company?
- will service within an associated company be counted?
- will breaks in service be ignored?
- will service be calculated in accordance with the statutory provisions, ie schedule 13 of the EP(C)A (see Appendix 2).

Attendance and Timekeeping

These two will require careful assessment of the accuracy and reliability of the available records and a fair analysis of absence levels, eg an employee may have a high level of absence due to illness in the months preceding selection, but an overall pattern of very low absenteeism.

Disciplinary Warnings

These will also need careful checking, eg are they still "live", subject to appeal, etc.

Job Performance — Contribution to the Business

This is a broad description that will need breaking down into skill levels, knowledge, experience, flexibility, appraisal records, productivity, supervisor's ratings, etc. The more subjective assessments can be avoided or balanced with more objective analyses, the sounder the selection will be. Constraints such as older machinery, supply problems and seasonal variations should be recognised.

Selection Criteria that are Discriminatory

The application of certain criteria can result in disproportionate numbers of employees of one sex or race being selected, and may render the subsequent dismissals unlawful.

The selection of part-timers first, for example, may constitute indirect sex discrimination if the majority of part-timers are women and the majority of full-timers male. Alternatively, if certain categories of jobs on the shop-floor have traditionally been filled by certain ethnic minorities, the employer may have to justify the criteria used at tribunal in order to refute claims of indirect race discrimination if the criteria have resulted in the dismissals of more employees from one particular ethnic minority than others.

The extent to which criteria used to produce a discriminatory effect can be justified objectively is still in question. In *Brook v Haringey Borough Council* (1992) IRLR 478, women were newcomers to the works department and disproportionately affected when LIFO was applied. In the EAT's view, LIFO had been agreed after lengthy consultation with the union and ACAS, and its effectiveness in achieving objective selection outweighed any discriminatory effects. This decision has been challenged and it will be useful to hear whether the Court of Appeal considers that the justification in this case meets the requirements cited by the ECJ and the House of Lords, eg *James v Eastleigh Borough Council* (1990) IRLR 288. The task of convincing a tribunal that discriminatory effects can be justified is now far harder, and an employer needs to consider very carefully whether in fact these effects are best avoided altogether. There is now no limit to the tribunal award for sex discrimination.

Claims of Discrimination with Collective Agreements

As a result of the TURERA, there is now provision within the **Sex Discrimination Act 1986** for employees and prospective employees to complain to a tribunal that rules or terms of a collective agreement have a potentially discriminatory effect. The tribunal can declare the term or rule void on these grounds. No compensation is payable.

Consultation

The principles set down by the EAT in *Williams and Others v Compair Maxam Ltd* (1982) IRLR 83 included "the employer will seek to ensure that the selection is made fairly in accordance with these criteria and will consider any representations the union may make as to such selection". The principles appear to be aimed at large employers with trade unions, rather than having a more general application. The EAT commented quite recently that the principles should not be elevated to the status of a statute — s.57(3) of the EP(C)A 1978 gave tribunals the scope to decide what was reasonable. The employer in *Rolls Royce Motor Cars Ltd v Price and others* EAT 1993 IRLR 203 had argued that the lack of individual consultation was not unreasonable as the *Compair-Maxam* principles did not require consultation with both the union *and* the employee. In the EAT's view, this was not a reliable interpretation. It was found that the employer had failed to consult reasonably because once the union had refused to agree the criteria, consultation stopped. In the EAT's view, Rolls Royce should have attempted consultation again when it was time to discuss how the criteria would be applied in practice.

The House of Lords' ruling in *Polkey v A E Dayton Services* (see Chapter 7) means that failure to consult employees on an individual basis on any aspect of their dismissal is likely to be unfair.

Appeals Procedure

The ACAS guide recommends that employers adopt a redundancy appeals procedure to hear complaints from employees who feel they have been unfairly selected.

Common Questions

Q.   The new Deregulation Bill published in January 1994 includes provision to repeal s.59(1)(b) of the EP(C)A. Does this mean selection agreements are no longer necessary?

A.   *The Bill proposes to remove breaches of agreed procedures and customary arrangements from the reasons that qualify as grounds for automatically unfair dismissal. There is currently provision for these departures from procedure to be justified by "special reasons", and increasing numbers of employers have departed from LIFO with an adequate "special reason". Even when s.59(1)(b) is deleted, employers will still need to show that the dismissal was reasonable within s.57(3). To breach a previously agreed selection procedure without adequate consultation could constitute unfair dismissal, and therefore procedures should be reviewed periodically to check their relevance to the needs of the business. The existence of a clear, fair, agreed selection agreement is conducive to good employee relations.*

Q. I have inserted a "no redundancies agreement" made with the trade union several years ago. Is this, as the union claims, an agreed procedure or selection?

A. *It is arguably not an agreement at all, but a commitment. It would be advisable to serve notice, if possible, that the commitment can no longer be adhered to and the reasons for this, but there is case law to support the view that an agreement procedure within s.59(1)(b) is an agreement on how to select for redundancy, and not an agreement not to select at all.*

Q. We are dismissing a 67 year old male employee as redundant. Is he due any payments? Our normal retirement age for all employees is 65?

A. *This employee is not entitled to a statutory redundancy payment, as eligibility is excluded at age 65. He may be entitled to a payment from a company scheme, ie a contractual redundancy payment, unless a similar proviso exists. If his pre-age 65 contract is still in operation, he will be due either his contractual notice entitlement or the statutory minimum, whichever is the greater. If he was re-employed after "retirement" at 65 on a temporary or fixed-term contract then the notice paid (or worked) will be the statutory minimum (ie 1–2 weeks) or the contractual provision, if this is greater.*

Figure 1: Redundancy Selection Assessment Form

Name: _____	Clock/staff no: _____
Job title: _____	Department: _____
Main duties: _____	

Criteria	Notes and Queries
Length of service	
Skills	
Experience	
Job knowledge	
Qualifications/training	
Effort	
Efficiency	
Attendance	
Timekeeping	
Disciplinary record	
Other factors	

Assessment/appraisal records checked (details): _____

_____

Signed: _____ Position: _____

7 A Reasonable Procedure

Introduction

The two main issues for employers to bear in mind are:
- consultation with the individual employee
- the possibility of suitable alternative employment.

Even in a unionised environment, consultation with the union(s) cannot entirely replace consultation with the individual. The EAT in *Wall's Meat Co Ltd v Selby* agreed with the employee's submission that two-tier consultation was necessary — first with the union and then with the individual. The Court of Appeal was unable to accept this proposition as binding on all employers, but nevertheless it has become established as good practice. The ACAS guidance booklet *Redundancy Handling* recommends that employees are consulted whether or not there are recognised trade unions, and irrespective of whether or not the individual is a member. ACAS suggests that employees who are consulted are more likely to react in a constructive way, and may be able to suggest alternatives to redundancy.

Consultation with the Individual Employee

The Industrial Relations Code of Practice made various recommendations about handling redundancies, including:
- giving as much warning of redundancy as practicable to the employee concerned
- consulting with employees on measures to avoid redundancy, eg short-time working, retraining or transfer to other work
- ensuring no public announcements are made before employees have been informed.

The Code was revoked in 1991, but its principles are now well enshrined in case law, most notably *Polkey v A E Dayton Services Ltd* (1987) IRLR 503.

Polkey v A E Dayton Services Ltd (formerly Edmund Walker (Holdings) Ltd) (1987) IRLR 503

Mr Polkey was a van driver and was dismissed as redundant without consultation or notice. The industrial tribunal, the EAT and the Court of Appeal all ruled that the dismissal was fair, on the basis that, although the employer had not followed a fair procedure, this did not affect the outcome, ie Mr Polkey would still have been dismissed. The House of Lords ruled that Mr Polkey had been unfairly dismissed. In their opinion it was the employer's actions at the time that had to be considered, rather than any speculation regarding what might have happened had the employer acted differently. A dismissal without consultation could only be fair if the employer, at the time of dismissal, had considered whether or not to consult and decided it would be "completely worthless".

As a result of *Polkey*, there has been greater emphasis on consultation and the importance of following agreed procedures. Quite how the test of what was in the employer's mind at the time of dismissal should be applied was considered by the EAT in *Duffy v Yeomans and Partners Ltd* (1993) IRLR 368. In this case the EAT held that the test was an objective one, ie could a *reasonable* employer, in the light of what was known at the time, have decided to dismiss without consultation? The employee appealed to the Court of Appeal. The Court rejected the appeal, holding that the tribunal was not wrong to find the dismissal fair when there had been no deliberate decision on the part of the employer that consultation would be useless. There were no grounds to say that there had to be such a deliberate decision by the employer. Nor were there grounds to say that a finding by a tribunal that the dismissal for redundancy was reasonable when there was no evidence of the employer making such a decision had to be wrong. Neither the legislation nor the *Polkey* decision supported such a finding.

The issue for the tribunal was whether the dismissal fell within the hand of reasonable responses.

Although this decision has diluted the requirement to consult, it is still advisable for the employer to consult prior to carrying out the redundancy.

Why the Emphasis on Consultation?

No communication with the employee means no discussion about suitable alternative employment, and it is this failure which will render the dismissal unfair. The tribunal will decide what actions would have been reasonable in the circumstances and this will be reflected in the compensation.

Below are some examples.

- Mining Supplies (Longwall) Ltd v Baker (1988) IRLR 417

  The tribunal awarded six weeks' pay as a compensatory award when Mr Baker, a toolmaker, was made redundant with no consultation. The employers argued that a six week period for individual consultation was excessive; the EAT ruled that two weeks was acceptable and reduced the compensatory award.

- Red Bank Manufacturing Co Ltd v Meadows (1992) IRLR 209

  Mr Meadows had 32 years' service when he was made redundant with no consultation. The tribunal calculated the compensatory award as being the difference between what he would have received had he continued with his old employer and his actual earnings since dismissal. The EAT remitted the case to tribunal for further consideration: the tribunal's approach was incorrect as *Polkey* requires tribunals to consider two questions:

  - if there had been consultation, would suitable alternative employment have been offered?

- if so, what would it have been, and what would the earnings have been?

- Croydon Advertiser Group v Clinton EAT 468/91

  Mrs Clinton, an advertising manager, was handed a letter on 23 July 1990 telling her that she must leave immediately and return on 27 July 1990 for a final interview. At this interview she asked to be re-engaged as a telesales assistant, but her employers considered this inappropriate. At tribunal, the employer submitted that the meeting on 27 July constituted consultation and the refusal to accept Mrs Clinton's suggestion was a reasonable response. At the EAT, the employer restated this view and also contended that the compensatory award should be significantly reduced to reflect the fact that Mrs Clinton would not have been re-engaged in telesales. The EAT's decision was that the tribunal was correct to decide that no meaningful consultation was possible after the letter given on 23 July. If there had been adequate consultation Mrs Clinton would have been appointed to telesales and therefore there should be no reduction in compensation.

What is Adequate Consultation?

Essentially, this depends on the circumstances. Small employers who have little scope for offering alternative employment will have more justification for curtailing consultation than associated companies or large public sector organisations. The requirement to consult is not removed, but it can be shorter and less formal. In *Ferguson v Prestwick Circuits Ltd* (1992) IRLR 266, the EAT stated that the employer must consult irrespective of the views of the workforce (the employer claimed that in a previous batch of redundancies employees had said they would have preferred to have been told on the day).

Given that the employer may have to demonstrate to a tribunal that consultation was considered at the time dismissals became unavoidable but was rejected as futile, and the *Polkey* case requires exceptional circumstances to justify this, a decision not to consult at all will need very careful consideration.

What is Meaningful Consultation?

This is an exchange of views between employer and employee, with the aim of listening to the views and information each has to give and exploring the options available.

It is always advisable to keep notes of all discussions and interviews, and the following checklist for discussion could be adapted to serve as a record of the discussion(s) that take place.

Checklist: A Guide to Meaningful Consultation

The employer should:

- explain why redundancies are necessary
- explain why the employee has been selected
- produce documentation, as appropriate
- explain why no suitable alternative work is currently available
- explain requirements during notice period (ie normal working, part or full time, pay-in-lieu, overtime, etc) and explain time-off provisions.*

*There is a statutory entitlement to time off for job searching or retraining for employees under notice of redundancy (see Appendix 7).

Suitable Alternative Employment

As discussed earlier, the possibility of suitable alternative employment requires serious consideration and adequate discussion. Points to bear in mind are that:

- the current contract may already contain a broad enough job title or mobility or flexibility clause for alternative work to fall within the scope of what the employee can reasonably be required to do — and therefore the transfer to new duties can occur without any need for notice or a trial period

- dismissal should be delayed if it is anticipated that opportunities are likely to occur shortly, eg due to high turnover or new orders

- the employee must be given enough information about the alternative job, and enough time, to make a sensible decision, and should be encouraged to take up a trial period

- reasonable efforts must be made to identify suitable vacancies within the company/organisation and also other associated companies/organisations or subsidiaries

- the employer should not assume that jobs which involve a drop in pay or status or which appear less attractive for other reasons will be unacceptable — they must still be discussed with the employee

- if the employee's performance during the trial period leads the employer to decide the new job is not suitable, the employer can dismiss and the dismissal date and the reason for the dismissal revert to the original termination date. The statutory redundancy payment will still be due. This dismissal will be subject to the s.57(3) provisions, ie it must be done fairly and reasonably or the employee will have grounds to claim unfair dismissal

- if the reason for dismissal is not connected with, or arising out of, the change in employment, eg misconduct, then the dismissal date and reason for dismissal do not revert back to the original termination, and eligibility for a redundancy payment is lost. The s.57(3) provisions will also apply in these circumstances (see above)

- employees absent on maternity leave must be considered for suitable alternative employment from the time the job they took leave from is made redundant, until the time at which they exercise the right to return, ie throughout maternity leave. *Philip Hodges & Co v Kell* 1994 IRLR 569.

Record Keeping

If a trial period is arranged, a note should be kept of when it will expire and the employee's performance in the new job.

Transferred Redundancy

More commonly known as "bumping" this arises when an employee not in the original pool of selection is dismissed to produce a job for another redundant employee.

There are two possibilities:

(a) an employee claims an alternative job *should* have been created by bumping, and claims unfair dismissal

(b) the "bumped" employee claims unfair dismissal.

As regards (a), the tribunal will decide each claim on an individual basis, purely on the facts of the case. The matter may have been raised and rejected during consultation and, if so, the employer should give this in evidence.

As regards (b), the employer needs to consider the implications carefully before "bumping". Although case law (particularly *W Gimber and Sons Ltd v Spurrett* (1967) ITR 308) confirms that the reason for the dismissal of the "bumped" employee will be the diminishing requirements of the business, ie redundancy, the contractual test for "work of a particular kind" (see Chapter 5) may mean that the "bumped" employee is *not* redundant because the need for his or her particular kind of work remains. If "bumping" does occur, it would be advisable to ensure that "bumped" employees are treated fairly and reasonably and to consider pleading "some other substantial reason" as well as "redundancy".

The Legal Remedies

A complaint of unfair dismissal must be referred to the industrial tribunal within three months of the effective date of termination. The effective date of termination is defined as:

- the date on which notice expires
- the date the dismissal took effect, if no notice was given
- the date on which a fixed-term contract expires.

The time limit can be extended if the tribunal considers it was not reasonably practicable for the claim to have been presented within three months.

If the dismissal is for taking official industrial action, the time limit is *six* months.

Some employees are excluded from the right to claim unfair dismissal (see Appendix 3).

If the tribunal finds the dismissal unfair, there are three remedies available, as follows:

• **Reinstatement:**	if the employee requests it and the tribunal considers it practicable. The return is to the old job. Arrears of pay, rights and privileges are due.
• **Re-engagement:**	if the employee requests it and the tribunal considers it practicable. The return is to a comparable job or a suitable alternative. Arrears of pay, rights and privileges are due.
• **Financial compensation consisting of:**	(a) a basic award (b) a compensatory award, and possibly (c) an additional award OR (d) a special award.

Basic award

If the employee received the correct statutory redundancy payment (ie a tribunal can make up the difference if there is a miscalculation) then no basic award is due. The basic award is calculated using the same method as redundancy payments (ie the maximum on a week's pay) with the exception that service under the age of 18 is also counted. There are four adjustments peculiar to redundancy dismissals:

(a) the basic award is limited to two weeks' pay if the employee unreasonably refused alternative employment

(b) the basic award is limited to two weeks' pay if the employee has accepted an alternative job, but has claimed unfair dismissal from the old one

(c) if the employee is not entitled to a redundancy payment, there is a minimum basic award of two weeks' pay

(d) if the dismissal is unfair on the grounds of trade union membership or activities (TULR(C)A), or on health and safety grounds (TURERA) then the basic award will be a minimum of £2700 (reviewed annually in April).

Compensatory award

This is the amount the tribunal considers just and equitable. The tribunal will take into account:

(a) loss of net earnings between the date of termination and the date of the tribunal hearing (including overtime, bonuses, etc)

(b) future loss of earnings, eg to compensate for unemployment or a reduction in pay if the new job is not as well paid

(c) loss of rights, ie the employee has lost continuity of employment and has to re-acquire employment protection

(d) loss of fringe benefits, eg pension rights, company care, private health scheme.

If the employee was given a contractual redundancy payment exceeding the statutory requirement, the excess can be set against the compensatory award.

If compensation is also due under the Sex Discrimination or Race Relations Acts, then compensation can only be awarded once for the same loss, eg there cannot be double compensation for loss of earnings.

The compensatory award can be reduced to reflect:

- earnings from a new job
- *ex gratia* payments made on termination
- the employee's conduct, if it contributes to the dismissal (rare in redundancy cases).

The limit on the compensatory award is currently £11,000 (reviewed annually).

Note: Compensation for claims of unlawful sex and race discrimination are not subject to a financial limit.

Additional award

If the tribunal orders reinstatement or re-engagement and the employer refuses without adequate justification, the tribunal will order an addition of:

- between 13 and 26 weeks' pay (current maximum is £205 per week)
- between 26 and 52 weeks' pay if the dismissal was due to sex or race discrimination (current maximum is £205 per week).

Note: In circumstances where the employer has failed to comply with an order for re-engagement or reinstatement, and has failed to satisfy a tribunal that compliance was not practicable, from 30 August 1993 the dismissed employee will receive the full amount of back pay specified in the re-engagement or reinstatement order.

Special award

If the dismissal is on the grounds of trade union membership or activities or on health and safety grounds, the special calculation of the special award will depend on whether the tribunal ordered reinstatement/re-engagement.

If reinstatement/re-engagement is not ordered, one week's pay × 104 should be awarded or £13,400, whichever is the greater (subject to maximum of £26,800).

If reinstatement/re-engagement is ordered and the employer cannot justify refusal, one week's pay × 156 should be awarded or £20,100, whichever is the greater.

If the employee is excluded from the right to a redundancy payment, no special award can be made. The award can also be reduced due to contributory fault, which in redundancy dismissals could be if the employee acts in such a way as to prevent reinstatement or re-engagement, or unreasonably refuses the employer's job offer.

Following TURERA where an order for reinstatement or re-engagement is not fully complied with and the tribunal makes an award of compensation, this will ordinarily be subject to the statutory limit on the compensatory award. However, this limit may be exceeded if this is necessary to enable the award to reflect more fully the value of the arrears of pay, etc due under the terms of the reinstatement or re-engagement order. This is designed to ensure that, in a case where the arrears payable are substantial, the employer is not made financially better off by failing to comply with the order. Similar rules apply where the employer fails to comply at all with an order of reinstatement or re-engagement and an additional award is made separate to the basic and compensatory awards.

Note: the employee must ask for reinstatement or re-engagement, or the special award cannot be made.

Common Questions

Q. I thought that when an alternative job in a new location was offered, a radius of six miles from the old job could be used to assess suitability. Is this correct?

A. *There are no general rules that can be applied to "suitability" because each employee has to be assessed individually. A job move of 12 miles could be suitable for one employee because it brings work nearer to home, whilst a move of 2 miles could be unsuitable for another because there is no public transport. The extra travelling time may not affect suitability, but the employee's refusal could be reasonable if it makes domestic commitments impossible.*

Q. We have given notice of redundancy to 20 of our employees and have given them details of vacancies within our company at different sites and also within our associated company. We will interview any employee who expresses an interest in a vacancy and give him or her preference over other applicants. How long should we wait for applications from the redundant employees before interviewing other staff?

A. *If any of your employees claim unfair dismissal, it is likely that the method you are using to offer re-employment will not be considered adequate.*

If the employees have to apply for jobs in competition with other applicants, then it is likely that this will not be viewed as making an offer of suitable alternative work — particularly if interviews are still continuing once the termination date has passed. It would be advisable to reconsider the procedure for offering suitable alternative employment to decide who will be consulted first, what vacancy or vacancies will be offered and the procedure to be used when one employee has reasonably refused and the vacancy must be offered to another.

Q. We have an employee with eight years' service who has worked one week of a trial period and the job is clearly unsuitable. We want to dismiss him — do we have to pay notice as well as the redundancy payment?

A. *There is no statutory requirement to give notice during the trial period and it could be argued that the trial period is a four week fixed-term contract and therefore does not qualify for statutory minimum notice. If a fixed-term contract is issued specifically for the trial period this would certainly help support this view. Given however that re-employment within four weeks of the offer being made, as long as it was made before the original contract ended, constitutes continuous employment, there is, arguably, a right to notice if dismissal takes place during the trial period. On balance, it is advisable to issue a contract specifically for the trial period (ie a fixed-term contract). Employees who either worked their formal notice under the old contract or who were paid in lieu are unlikely to claim a second term of notice.*

8 Minimising the Impact

Introduction

Although redundancy may be inevitable, there is however a great deal the employer can do to minimise its impact on his or her employees. This need not be an entirely selfless act, since remaining employees will take comfort in recognising that their employer is concerned with their welfare in even the worst circumstances. The employer can:

- encourage volunteers
- find less painful alternatives to unemployment, and
- soften the blow to the people affected.

We will consider each in turn.

Encouraging Volunteers

Advertise

The very first action to take is to advertise openly for volunteers. This is never a wasted activity, first because it is seen to be fair and second, because there is no telling who might volunteer or for what reason. Provided the employee who volunteers is not coerced and is seemingly aware of his or her action, the application should be treated positively because it will probably save the job of someone else who is wishing to remain employed.

Whoever volunteers and the reason behind this may be of interest, but are not important. Obviously it would be wrong to lose in this way an employee whose skills are critical for the survival of the business, but otherwise every effort should be made to accept the volunteer.

Incentive Terms

The flow of volunteers may be accelerated by offering enhanced severance terms for a limited period. Employees will have the option of leaving on these terms or risking being made redundant with less compensation. The device is not as mercenary as it might at first seem: employees who are anxious to retain their jobs will not be tempted, whilst those who, for whatever reason, find a lump sum of money more attractive than their current job will volunteer quickly. The extra cost of compensation can be weighed against the time and trouble of selecting people for redundancy, quite apart from the relief it offers to all parties.

Offer Contract Work

Some jobs may become redundant because there is insufficient work for a full-time employee. All employees affected will probably be very aware of this already and will be concerned. The blow of redundancy will therefore be anticipated, but its impact could be softened by offering them contract work as it becomes available. You may be able to guarantee a certain amount of work over a given period, though this arrangement should be realistic to avoid building false expectations. You may choose to enhance their severance pay if you feel it appropriate and circumstances so allow.

Encourage Self-employment

Whether or not you are able to offer them work, some employees may readily accept the employer's assistance in setting up their own businesses. This offer may be taken up by individuals who have a marketable skill or by groups of employees who believe they could operate more successfully together. In some circumstances the employer may be able to persuade employees from a whole department to set up business for themselves, in which case you may be the party who needs the guarantee of their availability! Accountants, company secretaries, marketing staff, personnel officers and technicians are all people who have successfully entered the world of self-employment and found it deeply satisfying. They can retain strong and mutually useful bonds with supportive ex-employers, yet enjoy freedom and a new sense of purpose in their lives.

The employer can offer help to these people in two ways: first by offering access to in-house facilities during their early days, eg printing, typing and photocopying, as well as a controlled amount of assistance from expert staff such as personnel, marketing, sales, advertising and accountancy executives. Second, the ex-employer could arrange for them to receive advice from outsiders such as solicitors or bankers; also perhaps offering loans to buy equipment — including business machines, furniture, plant — or paying for a college start-up course or a mail shot. Appropriate assistance will depend upon the individuals and the type of business involved.

Many employees might be frustrated businessmen and women who are reluctant to plunge into uncertainty. Surrendering a secure job, especially during a recession, may seem foolhardy, but if the job itself is threatened, security disappears and self-employment becomes an attractive alternative. The message of redundancy could bring a reaction of terror and relief; by focusing on the latter you could introduce a very efficient means of carrying out redundancy without damaging the people affected.

Early Retirement

Among the volunteers for redundancy there are likely to be people who are close to retirement. They may welcome the opportunity of avoiding the long haul of the last few working years; they may feel that their pension, albeit reduced, is adequate or they may have pangs of conscience about depriving younger workers with new families of their incomes. These applications must be treated positively, though you need to examine their motivation and circumstances to ensure that they are not imposing an unfair burden upon themselves.

However, regardless of who might volunteer, it is well worth looking at the financial circumstances of any employee who is within two or three years of retirement. It is useful to produce a set of calculations for each employee showing the benefit to the employee and employer both by remaining at work until retirement and by leaving now or in the near future. The chart below shows some of the factors that might be taken into account, and how they may be compared.

	Employee's income (until normal retirement date)	Employer's cost
Employee remains	Net salary/Other valuable benefits.	Gross salary/Benefits/ Pension contributions/ NI contributions/ Other employee costs.
Employee leaves	Redundancy pay/Pay in lieu of notice/Other severance payments. Early pension for x months/State benefits.	Redundancy pay/Pay in lieu of notice/Other severance payments/ Top-up pension payment.

Some of these factors may be inappropriate, others may need adding. The employer can also involve the appropriate government agency to determine eligibility for and level of State benefit; unemployment benefit, for example, will depend among other things upon the employee's contribution record and the early pension arrangements.

All of this may be too much for an elderly employee to grasp and it may be better to use a non-involved advisor to explain the situation to the employee, ensuring that it is understood and checking that there are no relevant personal factors that have been overlooked. The advisor could also ensure that the employee is not being, and does not feel, coerced.

Alternatives to Unemployment

Retrain for Other Work

Some employees selected for redundancy might have no interest in self-employment or retirement. They may also have poor chances of early re-employment in their existing work. If there are any vacancies for which employees could be trained, it would be prudent to give them an assessment and, if suitable, determine how best they might be given appropriate training. If appropriate, the employee's right to a four week trial period may be extended by written agreement.

Sponsor Further Education

An employee who does not have heavy financial commitments may use redundancy as a spur to gain further qualifications or to make a career change by undertaking long-term full-time further education. Quite commonly MBA students are mature people funded by redundancy payments, who are looking to enhance their prospects of securing senior management appointments. Other people take the opportunity of training to be welders, HGV drivers, computer repairers and any employment where vacancies exist and training is available.

The local Jobcentre should be contacted to give people information about training opportunities, offer them help and guidance and give advice about available grants from the State and other sources.

Sabbaticals

If you believe that demand for certain employees may return after a period, encouraging staff to think of taking a sabbatical may be appropriate.

Some people may be prepared to go away — to travel abroad or to go to college — for an extended period if they are assured that you will do your best to re-employ them on their return. This cushioning is largely psychological: it can apply only to people who can afford to give up work for a while and offers guarantees to neither party, but it does signal clearly that redundancy has been brought about by business circumstances and not by the individual's performance.

Helping the Employees

Earlier in this book we explained the duties the law imposes upon the employer to notify and consult with employees affected by redundancy in order to obviate or reduce the impact of redundancy. However, there is more that you can, and indeed should, do to help your people through this distressing experience.

Notify the Press

A well prepared press statement can achieve several useful purposes. It can break the news and give the reason for the redundancy in a way you would wish, for example because of a restructuring to make the business more competitive, rather than because you are going to the wall. More usefully for the employees, it can tell other employers in the area that there are available employees who are particularly skilled or experienced and who are likely to be available in the immediate future.

Circulate Other Employers

As soon as you have informed those employees who are to be made redundant you should compile lists showing their qualifications, experience and particular skills and strengths. A short descriptive paragraph on each person is much warmer and of greater use than a one-line entry on a list. Ask each employee to write or check his or her entry as he or she may have skills you do not know about.

Circulate these lists to:

- employers in the area
- employers in the same business
- customers and suppliers
- employers' associations
- local chambers of commerce
- trade unions
- professional associations
- anyone else you can think of who may be able to give employment to any of the employees on the list.

You cannot overdo this exercise. Once the list is compiled, each recipient (or potential source of re-employment) costs the price of a first class stamp.

Use the Department of Employment

A key role of the Department of Employment (DE) is to find work for the unemployed. They have considerable latitude in how they go about this. Therefore as soon as you recognise that you will have to declare redundancies call the local manager, explain the problems and ascertain what help is available.

Given adequate notice, and subject to demands on their resources, DE staff are likely to be prepared to visit affected employees at their workplace to explain unemployment benefit rights, claims procedures, training opportunities and grants, and to answer employees' questions. Some of this work may be done in conjunction with the Department of Social Security (DSS).

Additionally, the DE may make arrangements for you to be notified of new vacancies as they arise so that employees may make prompt and direct applications.

Appoint a member of staff, eg a personnel officer, to maintain liaison with these outside bodies and ensure that they are allowed to give employees the best possible service.

Outplacement Assistance

This assistance aims to equip redundant people to find appropriate alternative work efficiently. The help is likely to include:

- counselling, to deal with the immediate trauma and help people come to terms with redundancy
- advice about handling finances once income is cut off
- in-depth interviewing to help the employee recognise his or her real strengths and weaknesses, likes and dislikes, and true ambitions
- psychometric testing to support the interviews
- production of a CV and training in writing applications
- advice on the best means of seeking out vacancies and how best to apply for them
- interviewing training and practice
- development of assertiveness skills to help maintain confidence.

This work is normally carried out by specialist employment or outplacement consultants, but there is no reason why suitably trained personnel staff should not carry it out. Some of the work calls for individual attention, but the training sessions can usefully and economically be provided for groups of employees.

This chapter contains the most commonly used means of softening the blow of redundancy. However, it does not purport to be exhaustive. Redundancy is a very personal experience — certainly for the individual made redundant, but also for the employer. Some employees may handle it well, others just cannot cope. Some might take it as a signal of personal failure, others are more philosophical or even treat it as a minor problem. Only the employer who knows his or her employee well can read how the redundant employee is likely to react.

9 Redundancy Payments

Introduction

Compensation for employees who are dismissed as redundant was introduced by the **Redundancy Payments Act 1965**.

The facility for employers to claim a rebate from the State was eventually abolished altogether by the **Wages Act 1986**, except for small employers (nine employees or fewer on the relevant date).

Employers may agree to pay over and above the statutory entitlement. Receipt of a redundancy payment does not bar the employee from subsequently claiming unfair dismissal. The redundancy payment will normally offset the basic award, however, if the claim succeeds and the compensatory award will be reduced to reflect the balance between the statutory entitlement and the employer's contractual payment (*ex gratia* payments are discussed in Common Questions on page 115.

Exceptions

Dismissal on the grounds of redundancy does not automatically confer entitlement to a payment. Employees can be or become excluded for a variety of reasons:

- continuous service
- retirement age
- waiver clause in fixed-term contract
- the work is outside Great Britain
- misconduct
- strikes
- specific categories

- suitable alternative employment
- previous redundancy payment.

Continuous Service

To qualify for a redundancy payment, the employee must have 2 years' continuous service (regardless of the number of hours worked).

Service with an associated employer will count as will service with a previous employer if the business was transferred within the TUPE (see Chapter 4).

Gaps in employment can also count, if the break was caused by:
- sickness and/or pregnancy
- a temporary cessation of work
- custom or arrangement
- dismissal and subsequent re-engagement/reinstatement.

Further details are given in Appendix 2.

Age

The employee must be either under 65 or have reached the normal retirement age for a person in that position in the organisation. If the normal retirement age is not below 65, the cut-off point will be 65. The normal retirement age must be non-discriminatory, ie the same for men and women. Service below the age of 18 does not count for redundancy pay purposes.

Fixed-term Contracts

The **Employment Protection (Consolidation) Act 1978** (EP(C)A) defines the expiry of a fixed-term contract as a dismissal (see Chapter 4). If the contract was for two years or more or together with previous contracts gives overall qualifying service of two years or more then the employee may be entitled to a redundancy payment. The reason for the dismissal must still fit the statutory definition of redundancy.

If, however, the employee signed a waiver clause excluding the right to claim a redundancy payment and this has not been invalidated (see Chapter 4) then the entitlement has been lost.

Employment Outside Great Britain

Great Britain is defined as England, Wales, Scotland, British territorial waters and certain offshore installations! The employee must be in Great Britain on the *relevant date* (see page 106) to qualify for a redundancy payment. If this is not the case, the employee can still qualify if the work is "ordinarily in Great Britain". This can be a difficult question to answer and needs to be defined either by what the contract says or by ascertaining the employee's base throughout the contract. The base can be determined using such factors as:

- the location of headquarters
- where the travels for the purpose of employment begin and end
- where the employee's private residence is
- where, and in what currency, salary payments are made
- in which country National Insurance contributions are paid.

An employee who ordinarily works outside Great Britain but is in Great Britain on the relevant date may also qualify for a redundancy payment.

Misconduct

If an incident of gross misconduct occurs whilst an employee is under notice of redundancy and the employee is dismissed because of this, then entitlement to a redundancy payment is lost.

The employer may dismiss without notice or dismiss giving all or part of the notice due; as long as the offence constitutes gross misconduct the redundancy payment can be withheld. If full notice is given, there is a statutory requirement to give the employee a written statement saying that the employee has been dismissed for gross misconduct, and that the employer could have dismissed without notice. **Note:** it is probably always advisable to supply the employee with a written explanation.

As long as the dismissal has occurred in "the obligatory period" (see Chapter 4), the employee can present a claim for a redundancy payment to an industrial tribunal, within three months of the termination date.

The tribunal will decide whether any redundancy payment should be awarded and, if so, whether it is paid in full, eg in *Lignacite Products Ltd v Krollman* (1979) IRLR 23 the EAT agreed that an employee with 24 years' service dismissed for stealing whilst under notice of redundancy should receive 60% of his redundancy pay.

Strikes

Employees who take part in a strike during the redundancy notice period and who are subsequently dismissed for gross misconduct do not lose their right to a redundancy payment, as long as their strike action and the dismissal occurred in the obligatory period. Entitlement will be lost if:

- the dismissal is for industrial action, eg working to rule or an overtime ban, and not strike action
- the strike took place before the obligatory period started.

The written statement requirement that applies to gross misconduct dismissals also applies to strike action dismissals, ie if full notice is given, there must be a written statement indicating that in fact no notice need have been given.

The employer can serve a *notice of extension* to striking employees. This requires them to work beyond the original notice in order to make up the days lost by the strike. The notice of extension must:

- give the reasons for wanting the extension
- state that unless the employee complies (ie gives acceptable reasons for not doing so) the redundancy payment will be withheld and can be served before the obligatory period begins.

An industrial tribunal will hear claims from employees in these circumstances and can award full or part payment, as it thinks fit.

Specific Categories

The following are excluded:

- crown servants
- the self-employed
- agency employees
- share fishermen
- employees covered by an *exemption order* granted by the Secretary of State, ie an agreement between an employer or employer's organisation and a trade union or unions that certain payments will be made on termination of employment. There must be provision within the agreement for questions arising from it to be referred by either party to an industrial tribunal.

Suitable Alternative Employment

The offer of alternative employment will result in the loss of a redundancy payment if the offer is either accepted or unreasonably refused. The offer does not have to be in writing, but it must:

- be made before the original contract ends
- be an offer to renew the original contract or to re-engage under a new contract. The renewal or re-engagement must occur either immediately the original contract ends or not more than four weeks afterwards.

If an offer of alternative employment is *accepted*, the employee may be entitled to a statutory trial period (see page 103).

If an offer is *refused*, then the employer has the option to withhold the redundancy payment. Claims to an industrial tribunal will be assessed in terms of:

- the suitability of the offer
- the reasonableness of the refusal.

Suitability

If the job offered by either the old employer or an associated employer is on the same terms as the old contract, particularly as regards place and capacity, then the employee has fairly limited grounds on which to reasonably refuse — if a new job has already been found with another company for example, then this would probably constitute a reasonable refusal.

If the job is on different terms, it must be "substantially equivalent". Tribunals assessing suitability have taken account of changes in pay, status and loans, and looked at the aptitude and capabilities of the employee. In *STC Ltd v Yates* (1981) IRLR 21 the job offered was unsuitable because it was less skilled. The question is one of fact, to be determined with regard to the work previously done by the individual employee. In *Hindes v Supersine Ltd* (1979) IRLR 343 the EAT ruled that a drop in pay of £10.00 per week meant the new job was not suitable and that the test was an objective one, ie on the facts presented, is the new job suitable when compared to the old?

Reasonableness

If the employee refuses the offer, however, the test for reasonableness is a subjective one, and must take into account the employee's personal circumstances. For example:

- the care of children or elderly relatives, or the need to fit in with a partner's shift arrangements could make certain journeys or start and finish times unacceptable

- the employee could reasonably refuse if the standards required in the new job are seen as unachievable (*Spencer and Griffen v Gloucs County Council* (1985) IRLR 393)
- in *Cambridge and District Co-Op Society Ltd v Ruse* (1993) IRLR 156, the manager of a butcher's shop was offered a job in charge of the butchery department within a supermarket. The EAT decided that the new job was suitable, but confirmed that reasonableness must be assessed subjectively, and that the drop in status meant that his refusal was reasonable and therefore redundancy pay was due.

Statutory trial period

If the alternative job offered is different from the previous job, either "wholly or in part", then the employee has a statutory right to a trial period. This gives the employee the opportunity to try out the new job before deciding whether or not it is suitable, and provides him or her with the possibility of still leaving with a redundancy payment.

The trial period must begin when the old contract ends and lasts for four weeks. The new job must begin not more than four weeks after the end of the old contract and the right to retain entitlement to a redundancy payment only applies to trial periods of four weeks or less (four weeks = four consecutive calendar weeks). The only exception to this is if the trial period is for the purpose of retraining.

Note: Trying out the new job whilst still working under the old contract is not a statutory trial period, but a common law trial period. An employee who agrees to a common law trial period is still entitled to a statutory trial period (see Chapter 4).

The extended trial period

If a longer trial period for retraining is required a written agreement between the employer and the employee/employee representative must be finalised before work under the new contract begins. The agreement must specify:

- the date the trial period will end
- the terms and conditions of employment which will apply to the employee after the end of the trial period.

Multiple trial periods

The employee is not limited to one trial period — if the employer agrees the employee can try out a variety of jobs.

Resignation during the trial period

The employee must terminate the contract or give notice to terminate it during the trial period. If the employer considers the new job suitable *and* the employee's departure unreasonable, or is not prepared to agree the alternative was unsuitable, then the redundancy payment can be withheld.

Note: the employee can leave for any reason, but the entitlement is at risk if the employee leaves unreasonably, eg too hastily.

The employee must refer the claim to the industrial tribunal which will apply the tests of suitability and reasonableness mentioned earlier. If the employer does not contest the resignation, the employee is entitled to redundancy pay based on the service accrued under the original contract, ie the reason for the dismissal is redundancy and the date of dismissal is the date the original contract ended.

Dismissal during the trial period

It can become apparent fairly quickly that the new job is not suitable, or presents too many difficulties to make it a feasible option. The employer should consider whether there are any other alternatives available, but can proceed to terminate or give notice to terminate withih the four week trial period and the entitlement to redundancy pay will remain, ie the date of dismissal is the date the original contract ended, and the reason for dismissal is redundancy.

As mentioned earlier, paying the redundancy compensation does not prevent the employee claiming unfair dismissal, and a tribunal will still apply the tests of fairness and reasonableness to a dismissal during a trial period (*Hempell v W H Smith and Sons Ltd* (1986) IRLR 95).

If the dismissal is not for a reason connected with or arising out of the change to the new contract, eg the employee has been dismissed for misconduct, then:

- the right to a redundancy payment is lost
- the termination date is the date the dismissal during the trial period takes effect.

A Previous Redundancy Payment

Schedule 13, paragraph 12 of the EP(C)A contains provision for the payment of a statutory redundancy payment to break continuity for the purposes of calculating future redundancy payments, ie the employee cannot receive more than one redundancy payment for the same period of service. There are various circumstances in which this could happen, for example;

- the employee is re-employed, and the continuity is preserved by virtue of either temporary cessation of work or custom and/or arrangement (see Appendix 2)
- the gap is less than one week and therefore continuity is not broken, eg a transfer between associated employers.

The effect of schedule 13, paragraph 12 is that the employee's overall service, including the gap, will count for the purposes of statutory minimum notice and unfair dismissal rights, but the redundancy payment will only be calculated on service accrued after the termination of the original contract.

Redundancy Pay

This is calculated in accordance with the rules in schedule 4 of the EP(C)A. The calculation is based on the length of continuous employment and the employee's age (see page 108). The point of reference is what is known as the *relevant date*.

Defining the Relevant Date

- If the employee's contract is terminated with notice, the relevant date is the date on which the notice expires.
- If the employee's contract is terminated without notice the relevant date is the date on which the termination takes effect.
- If the employee is employed under a fixed-term contract, the relevant date is the expiry date.
- If the employee resigns during the trial period, the relevant date is the same as it would have been under the original contract.
- If the employee resigns during the obligatory period (see page 35), the relevant date is the date the employee's notice expires.

Special Rules

If the employer fails to give the statutory minimum notice to which the employee is entitled (and any employee who has been employed for one month under a contract for 16 or more hours per week will qualify for notice) the relevant date is determined in one of two ways:

- if some notice was given, the relevant date is the date the statutory minimum notice would have expired, if it had been given on the same date that the actual notice was given
- if no notice was given, the relevant date becomes the date the statutory minimum notice would have expired if it had been given on the date that the employment was terminated.

The most common application of these special rules is to dismissals where money is paid in lieu of notice. These dismissals constitute "dismissals with no notice given". The special rules apply to:

  (i) calculating the qualifying period

  (ii) calculating continuous service

and are therefore of particular concern when dismissals without the statutory notice entitlement occur:

- immediately prior to the completion of two years' continuous employment

- immediately prior to the anniversary of the employee's start date

- immediately prior to the employees' 42nd birthday as their application will alter the payment due.

Continuous Employment

Continuous employment is worked out in accordance with schedule 13 of the EP(C)A and the relevant information for redundancy pay purposes is given in Appendix 2.

Age

Employment whilst under 18 will not count, and neither will service over the age of 65 *or* over the normal retiring age, if this is lower than 65.

When the relevant date falls between the 64th and 65th birthday, the payment is reduced by one-twelfth for each complete month over 64.

The Computation

The number of complete years is assessed by starting at the relevant date and counting backwards. Up to a maximum of 20 years can be counted.

> **Checklist: The information needed for calculating the payment due**
>
> There are various reference points and items of information to be collated for each employee:
>
> - the employee's date of birth
> - the date of commencement with this employer, an associated employer or a previous employer if covered by TUPE
> - the length of continuous employment
> - the relevant date
> - the calculation date
> - the weekly earnings ("a week's pay")
> - the pension arrangements.

For each year the employee was aged 41–64   1½ weeks' pay
For each year the employee was aged 22–40   1 week's pay
For each year the employee was aged 18–21   ½ week's pay.

A Week's Pay

The rules on calculating a week's pay are contained in schedule 14 of the EP(C)A. A week's pay is subject to a current maximum of £205 and is normally reviewed in April each year. The pay is calculated with reference to the calculation date. 1998 - £220.

Defining the Calculation Date

The way in which the contract was ended will determine the date as follows.

- If the entitlement to notice was the statutory minimum, and the full entitlement was given, then the calculation date is *the date on which statutory notice was given*.

- If there was an entitlement to contractual notice, that exceeded the statutory minimum, the calculation date is the date *on which the statutory notice would have been given* to end the contract on the relevant date. The calculation date is arrived at by counting backwards from the relevant date.

- If no notice was given, then the calculation date is brought forward to the relevant date, ie *the dates will be the same*.

- If the notice given falls short of the statutory minimum entitlement, the calculation date *is the date on which the notice expired*.

Defining the Week's Pay

The method used will depend on whether or not the employee works normal hours. This can be defined by the contract as well as what happens in practice.

- Does the written statement provide for basic hours and overtime once this number of hours is exceeded?
  - then the normal hours = the basic hours.

- Does the written statement provide for a fixed number of hours greater than the basic?
  - then some overtime* is guaranteed and the fixed hours = the normal hours.

*Note: the overtime must be guaranteed by the employer *and* be obligatory for the employee.

"What is a week?"

A week is a week ending with a Saturday, except in the case of an employee whose pay is calculated weekly by a week ending with a day other than a Saturday, in which case that day ends the week.

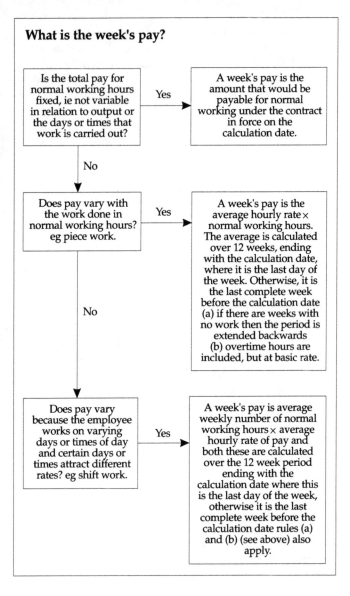

What is the week's pay?

Is the total pay for normal working hours fixed, ie not variable in relation to output or the days or times that work is carried out?	**Yes** →	A week's pay is the amount that would be payable for normal working under the contract in force on the calculation date.

No ↓

Does pay vary with the work done in normal working hours? eg piece work.	**Yes** →	A week's pay is the average hourly rate × normal working hours. The average is calculated over 12 weeks, ending with the calculation date, where it is the last day of the week. Otherwise, it is the last complete week before the calculation date (a) if there are weeks with no work then the period is extended backwards (b) overtime hours are included, but at basic rate.

No ↓

Does pay vary because the employee works on varying days or times of day and certain days or times attract different rates? eg shift work.	**Yes** →	A week's pay is average weekly number of normal working hours × average hourly rate of pay and both these are calculated over the 12 week period ending with the calculation date where this is the last day of the week, otherwise it is the last complete week before the calculation date rules (a) and (b) (see above) also apply.

What if there are no normal working hours?

The average weekly remuneration for the 12 week period is "a week's pay". If no pay was given for any of those weeks, the 12 weeks is extended backwards to include paid weeks. Overtime payments are included.

What if other payments fall outside the 12 week period?

Adjustments should be made to "fairly represent a week's pay". Commission, for example, should be computed to the annual amount, and then calculated *pro rata* to the 12 week period. Similarly, bonus payments should also be calculated *pro rata* to the 12 week period.

Offsetting pension

The **Redundancy Payments Pensions Regulations 1965** allow employers to offset payments under occupational pension schemes against redundancy payments. The details are complex and employers should consult the Employment Department's leaflet RLP1 *Offsetting pensions against redundancy payments*.

The provisions apply when:

- the pension scheme allows retirement below the age of 65 (eligibility for a statutory redundancy payment is excluded at age 65+)
- the pension is payable for life or is payable as a lump sum, and is not subject to termination or suspension except in unusual circumstances, eg imprisonment or re-engagement
- the pension scheme is approved by the Secretary of State for Employment
- the pension payments (whether lump sum and/or periodical payments) are to begin within 90 weeks of the employment terminating.

The whole of the redundancy payments can be offset if the annual value of the pension and/or lump sum is equal to one third or more of the employee's pay. (**Note**: the weekly limit — currently £205 applies *and* the pension and/or lump sum is payable within a week of termination.)

The formula used for calculating offset:

$$\frac{\text{Statutory redundancy payment due (before offset)} \times \text{the first year's pension payment} + \frac{1}{10} \text{ of any lump sum (where payable)}}{52 \times \text{a week's pay (current maximum £205 per week)} \times \frac{1}{3}}$$

The amount that can be offset is reduced as the interval between termination and pension payment increases.

Offset cannot be done if the pension payments are:

- made under the statutory social security scheme
- solely a return of the employee's own contributions
- part of a benefit solely attributable to voluntary additional contributions paid by the employee.

The employee must be given *written notice* of the offset, detailing the reduction and its calculation.

Every employee is entitled to a written statement setting out how the statutory redundancy payment was calculated.

An employer who fails to give a written statement, without a reasonable excuse, can be prosecuted and fined up to £200. Additionally, if the employee serves a written notice requiring the information and the employer fails to comply, and is found to have no reasonable excuse, the employer can be fined up to £1000. The employee can set a time limit on the reply, but it must be at least a week from the date of the notice.

Employees given a redundancy payment exceeding the statutory minimum are still entitled to a written statement for the statutory element. See figure 2 for sample letter on page 114.

The Legal Remedy

An employee can claim to an industrial tribunal on the grounds that there was a right to a redundancy payment and the employer refused to pay, or that the payment was incorrect.

Unlike unfair dismissal claims the tribunal will *presume* the dismissal was for redundancy, ie the burden of proof rests with the employer, who must contest the reason.

The employee has six months from the relevant date (which cannot be extended for this purpose if no notice or short notice was given) to refer the claim. During the six months, the employee must either:

- make a claim for redundancy pay in writing to the employer
- refer a claim for redundancy pay to an industrial tribunal
- present a claim of unfair dismissal to an industrial tribunal.

If a claim is not made within this time, a further six month period can be granted, if the industrial tribunal considers this is justified by the reasons given for the delay.

Figure 2: Sample written statement — statutory redundancy pay

Dear _____

As we discussed recently, I am writing to give you details of how your statutory redundancy payment has been calculated.

If you have any queries, please contact _____ who will be able to advise you.

The details regarding the calculation of your statutory redundancy payment are given below.

[Information regarding the contractual redundancy payment you are due will be given in a separate statement _____]

[Information regarding the contractual redundancy payment and *ex gratia* payment you will also receive will be given in a separate statement _____]

Statutory Redundancy Payment

1. The *relevant date* for the purpose of this calculation is _____ .

2. Total length of continuous employment (maximum 20 years) _____ .

3. Age, in complete years, at the relevant date _____ .

4. Number of weeks' pay due:

    _____ × ½

    *plus

    _____ × 1

    plus

    _____ × 1½

    = _____

    *see note below

5. Amount of a week's pay (maximum currently £205 per week) _____ .
6. Amount of redundancy payment due (4) × (5) _____ .
7. Deductions (delete as appropriate):
   (a) the redundancy payment is reduced by $\frac{1}{12}$ for each complete month between the 64th birthday and the termination date
   (b) pension payments due will be offset against the redundancy payment.

As a result of (a) and (b), the final amount of redundancy pay due is _____ .

This payment will be made to you on _____ . together with money in lieu of notice/your final wage/salary payment.

If there is anything you would like to discuss before you leave, please raise it with _____ .

*	For each year aged 18–21	$\frac{1}{2}$ week's pay
	For each year aged 22–40	1 week's pay
	For each year aged 41–64	$1\frac{1}{2}$ weeks' pay.

Common Questions

Q. We would like to make *ex gratia* payments to two senior managers, who may claim unfair dismissal (and we do not wish to discuss a COT3* or a compromise† settlement). Does the tribunal take account of *ex gratia* payments when assessing the award?

A. *Yes: as long as the payment is genuinely ex gratia, ie there is no contractual entitlement or "legitimate expectation", it can be deducted from the employee's total loss, before the statutory limit on the compensatory award is applied.*

Q. As a company, we pay generous redundancy pay well in excess of the statutory minimum. Is this taxable?

A. Payments to compensate for loss of employment are not taxable unless they exceed £30,000. The Inland Revenue has recently issued a new statement of practice, however, (SP1/94) which distinguishes terminal bonuses, eg payments made as an inducement to remain until closure or for undertaking extra duties during the notice period, as liable for tax. In view of these changes, it may be worth checking the implications of your scheme with the Inland Revenue in advance of any further redundancies.

Q. We have employed a nanny for three years who is no longer needed as our children are all at school. She has been told she is entitled to a redundancy payment. Is this correct?

A. Yes! She qualifies as a "domestic servant" and, unless she is also a close relative, she is not excluded from entitlement.

Q. An employee who is over 64 was made redundant and given six weeks' pay in lieu of notice. As this gave him another complete month's service over the age of 64, we deducted a further $\frac{1}{12}$ from his redundancy pay. Was this correct?

A. Unfortunately, no. The relevant date can only be extended for the purpose of calculating redundancy pay, not reductions. He is due that $\frac{1}{12}$ pay deducted.

Q. A pay award was given after the calculation date for some of our employees. Should we take that into account when calculating a week's pay?

A. No. Pay awards made after the calculation date and before termination do not affect the calculation, even if they are backdated.

Q. When an employee is dismissed as redundant, is there an interval during which they must not be re-employed?

A. *No. Any gap in employment may count for the purposes of continuous service (see Appendix 2). Service cannot be counted twice for the purposes of redundancy payments (see earlier), and there is no statutory provision requiring employees to repay their redundancy payments. Employees therefore are best advised to keep these payments — or at least the statutory element.*

*COT3 are agreements reached with the assistance of ACAS.

† Compromise settlements are agreements introduced by TURERA, reached without ACAS, but with assistance, for the employee, from an independent lawyer. (For further details see *Croner's Reference Book for Employers*.)

Glossary

ASSOCIATED EMPLOYERS   Any two employers are to be treated as associated if one is a company of which the other (directly or indirectly) has control, or if both are companies of which a third person (directly or indirectly) has control.

BUSINESS   Includes a trade or profession and includes any activity carried on by a body of persons whether incorporated or not.

COLLECTIVE AGREEMENT   Any agreement or arrangement made by or on behalf of one or more trade unions and one or more employers or employers' associations and relating to one or more of the matters specified below:

(a) terms and conditions of employment, or the physical conditions in which any workers are required to work

(b) engagement or non-engagement or termination or suspension of employment or the duties of employment of one or more workers

(c) allocation of work or the duties of employment as between workers or groups of workers

(d) matters of discipline

(e) the membership or non-membership of a trade union on the part of a worker

(f) facilities for officials of trade unions, and

(g) machinery for negotiation or consultation, and other procedures, relating to any of the above matters including the recognition by employers or employers' associations of the right of a trade union to represent workers in any such negotiation or consultation or in the carrying out of such procedures.

CONTRACT OF EMPLOYMENT

A contract of service or apprenticeship, whether express or implied and whether oral or in writing.

EFFECTIVE DATE OF TERMINATION

The date when the notice expires or, where no notice is given, the date of termination. However, if the statutory notice period is not given, the period of continuous employment is extended to the date when the notice would have expired for the purposes of qualifying service for rights to written statements for reasons for dismissal and to make a complaint of unfair dismissal and for the calculation of the basic award.

EMPLOYEE

An individual who has entered into or works under (or, where the employment has ceased, worked under) a contract of employment.

EMPLOYER

The person by whom the employee is (or, where the employment has ceased, was) employed.

EMPLOYMENT

Employment under a contract of employment, employment under a contract of service or apprenticeship or a contract personally to execute any work or labour.

INDEPENDENT TRADE UNION

A trade union which:

(a) is not under the domination or control of an employer or a group of employers or of one or more employers' associations, and

(b) is not liable to interference by an employer or any such group or association (arising out of the provision of financial or material support or by any other means whatsoever) tending towards such control.

JOB

In relation to an employee, this means the nature of the work which he or she is employed to do in accordance with the contract and the capacity and place in which he or she is so employed.

MONTH

In calculating continuous service, a month means one calendar month.

OFFER OF RE-ENGAGEMENT

An offer made by the original employer or a successor of that employer or an associated employer to re-engage an employee in the job he or she held immediately before dismissal or in reasonably suitable alternative employment.

OFFICIAL

Any person who is an officer of the union (ie a member of the governing body or trustee of any fund applicable for the purposes of the union) or of a branch or section of the union or also (not being such an officer) a person elected or appointed in accordance with the rules of the union to be a representative of its members or of some of them including any person so elected or appointed who is an employee of the same employer as the members or one or more of the members whom he or she has to represent.

POSITION In relation to an employee, this means the following matters taken as a whole, ie his or her status as an employee, the nature of his or her work and the terms and conditions of his or her employment.

RECOGNISED TRADE UNION A union which is recognised by the employer, to any extent, for collective bargaining purposes.

RELEVANT DATE For redundancy payment purposes, this is the date when notice expires or, if no notice is given, the date of termination, subject to three exceptions:

(a) where there has been a trial period, the relevant date is the date the original contract came to an end (other than for the purposes of claiming a redundancy payment)

(b) if the employee is redundant under the short-time working or lay-off provisions, the relevant date is the date on which the employee's notice to terminate expires, and

(c) if the statutory minimum notice is not given by the employer, the relevant date is extended to the date when the statutory notice would have expired for the purposes of calculating the qualifying service and the continuous service on which the redundancy payment is based.

RENEWAL Includes extension.

STRIKES OR OTHER INDUSTRIAL ACTION

The essential condition is that there must be a trade dispute. Any form of industrial action is covered, eg go-slows, overtime bans, working to rule, blacking, etc. The action need not necessarily be in breach of contract and it does not matter whether or not the action is in accordance with union rules.

SUCCESSOR

In relation to the employer of an employee, this means a person who, in consequence of a change occurring (whether by virtue of a sale or other disposition or by operation of law) in the ownership of the undertaking for the purposes of which the employee was employed, has become the owner of that undertaking or part of it as the case may be. This definition applies even where the owner before the change is not wholly different from the owner after the change (for example where there is a partial change in partners, trustees, etc).

TRADE DISPUTE

A dispute between workers and their employer which relates wholly or mainly to one or more of the following matters:

(a) terms and conditions of employment or the physical conditions in which any workers are required to work

(b) engagement or non-engagement or termination or suspension of employment or the duties of employment of one or more workers

(c) allocation of work or the duties of employment as between workers or groups of workers

(d) matters of discipline

(e) the membership or non-membership of a trade union on the part of a worker

(f) facilities for officials of trade unions, and

(g) machinery for negotiation or consultation, and other procedures, relating to any of the above matters including the recognition by employers or employers' associations of the right of a trade union to represent workers in any such negotiation or consultation or in the carrying out of such procedures.

TRADE UNION An organisation (whether temporary or permanent) which either:

(a) consists wholly or mainly of workers of one or more descriptions and is an organisation whose principal purposes include the regulation of relations between workers of that description or those descriptions and employers or employers' associations, or

(b) consists wholly or mainly of:

    (i) constituent or affiliated organisations which fulfil the above conditions, or

    (ii) representatives of such organisations

and whose principal purposes include the regulation of relations between workers and employers or employers' associations or include the regulation of relations between its constituent or affiliated unions.

WEEK   For the purposes of calculating a week's
pay means in relation to an employee
whose remuneration is calculated
weekly by a week ending with a day
other than a Saturday, a week ending
with that other day and in relation to
any other employee, a week ending with
a Saturday.

YEAR   A year of 12 calendar months.

Useful Addresses

Advisory, Conciliation and Arbitration Service (ACAS)

Head Office
27 Wilton Street
London SW1X 7AZ
Tel: 0171-210 3645

Regional Offices

Northern
Westgate House
Westgate Road
Newcastle upon Tyne NE1 1TJ
Tel: 0191-261 2191

Yorkshire and Humberside
Commerce House
St Albans Place
Leeds LS2 8HH
Tel: 0113 2431371

London
Clifton House
83–117 Euston Road
London NW1 2RB
Tel: 0171-396 5100

South Eastern
Westminster House
125 Fleet Road
Fleet GU13 8PD
Tel: 01252 811868

South Western
Regent House
27a Regent Street
Clifton
Bristol BS8 4HR
Tel: 0117 9744066

Midlands
Leonards House
319 Bradford Street
Birmingham B5 6ET
Tel: 0121-666 7576

North Western
Boulton House
17–21 Chorlton Street
Manchester M1 3HY
Tel: 0161-228 3222

Scotland
Franborough House
123–157 Bothwell Street
Glasgow G2 7JR
Tel: 0141-204 2677

Wales
Fourth Floor
Phase 1
Ty Glas Road
Llanishen
Cardiff CF4 5PH
Tel: 01222 762636

British Association of Counselling

1 Regent Place
Rugby CV21 2PJ
Tel: 01788 550899

Department of Employment

Head Office
Caxton House
Tothill Street
London SW1H 9NF
Tel: 0171-273 6969

Regional Offices

Eastern
Arena House
North End Road
Wembley HA9 0BS
Tel: 0181-903 8888

Midlands
2 Duchess Place
Hagley Road
Birmingham B16 8NS
Tel: 0121-456 1144

Northern
Broadacre House
Market Street East
Newcastle upon Tyne NE1 6HQ
Tel: 0191-232 6181

North West
Sunley Tower
Piccadilly Plaza
Manchester M1 4BE
Tel: 0161-832 9111

Southern
Unicorn House
28 Elmfield Road
Bromley BR1 1NX
Tel: 0181-464 6418

South West
The Pithay
Bristol BS1 2NQ
Tel: 0117 9273710

Yorkshire and Humberside
Jubilee House
33–41 Park Place
Leeds LS1 2RE
Tel: 0113 2446299

Scotland
Argyle House
3 Lady Lawson Street
Edinburgh EH3 9SD
Tel: 0131-229 9191

Wales
Companies House
Crown Way
Cardiff CF4 3UZ
Tel: 01222 388588

Industrial Tribunals (Central Offices)

England and Wales
The Secretary
Central Office of the Industrial Tribunals
100 Southgate Street
Bury St Edmonds IP33 2AQ
Tel: 01284 762300

Scotland
The Secretary
Central Office of the Industrial Tribunals
Saint Andrew House
141 West Nile Street
Glasgow G1 2RU
Tel: 0141-331 1601

Appendix 1 — Guarantee Payments

Calculation and Limits on Guarantee Payments

No guarantee payment is payable in respect of a day on which the employee has no normal working hours. Where payment is due it is calculated according to the following formula:

$$\text{Guarantee payment} = \text{number of normal working hours on the day in question} \times \text{guaranteed hourly rate}$$

Normal working hours means broadly the hours during which the employee is contractually required to be at work.

The guaranteed hourly rate (ghr) is calculated according to the following formula:

$$\text{ghr} = \frac{\text{one week's pay}}{\substack{\text{number of normal working hours in a week for} \\ \text{that employee under the contract of employment} \\ \text{in force on the workless day}}}$$

There are two exceptions. First, where the number of normal working hours varies from week to week, the guaranteed hourly rate is calculated as follows:

$$\text{ghr} = \frac{\text{one week's pay}}{\substack{\text{average normal working hours per week during} \\ \text{the 12 week period ending with the last complete} \\ \text{week before the workless day}}}$$

If the calculation cannot be made (because the employee has not been employed for a sufficient period) the denominator is the number which fairly represented the number of normal working hours in a week. Appropriate considerations are the average number of working hours which the employee could normally expect to work in accordance with the contract and the number of hours worked by other similar employees employed by the same employer.

Second, it may be that the contract of employment has been varied or a new contract entered into during a period of short-time working. If so, the above calculations are done as if the workless day was the last day on which the original contract was in force.

The maximum guarantee payment for any workless day is £14.10. This limit is reviewed annually by the Secretary of State for Employment in accordance with s.148 of the EP(C)A.

A further limitation is that an employee is not entitled to more than a specified number of guarantee payments in any period of three months. The specified number is the number of days on which the employee normally works in a week under the contract of employment in force on the day in respect of which the guarantee payment is claimed, subject to a maximum of five days in any three month period.

If the number of days worked in a week varies from week to week, then the average number of days is taken during the period of 12 weeks ending with the last complete week before the workless day. Where the average is not a whole number it is rounded up. The five day maximum applies here also. Once again, if the employee has not been employed for a sufficient period to make the calculation, a fair number is taken, taking into account the same considerations which apply to calculation of the guaranteed hourly rate. If a new contract is entered into as a result of short-time working, the original contract should be used for the purpose of calculation.

Statutory Payments and Contractual Remuneration

The right to a guarantee payment does not affect the right to contractual remuneration.

The rules are as follows.

1. Contractual remuneration paid in respect of a workless day goes towards the discharge of any liability to pay a guarantee payment. If the amount due under the contract is greater than the guarantee payment the right to the guarantee payment is extinguished. This applies, of course, only if the contractual remuneration is paid.
2. Any guarantee payment paid goes towards discharging any contractual remuneration due for the workless day.
3. Contractual remuneration is treated as paid in respect of a workless day:
    (a) if it is calculated or payable by reference to the workless day and in any other case
    (b) to the extent that it represents guaranteed remuneration for the workless day.

Under (b), where for example a contractual guarantee is paid on some basis other than a daily basis, then the amount paid (say for a week) may be apportioned on a daily basis.

For example, suppose that an employee is guaranteed £100 for 40 hours. He works four days and is laid off on the fifth but is entitled to £110 for the 32 hours worked. Contractually he is entitled to no guarantee pay for that week and will be entitled to a full statutory guarantee payment for the workless day. Alternatively, suppose that he had only been entitled to £95 for the work actually done. The make-up on the contractual guarantee would be £5 and that amount could be set against the statutory liability for the fifth day. Third, suppose that the employee was contractually entitled to £95 for three days, and there were two workless days, the make-up of £5 would be apportioned equally between the two workless days. If the employer was only bound to pay a guarantee payment for one of those days the full payment less £2.50 would be due.

Guarantee Pay and Statutory Sick Pay (SSP)

The relationship between guarantee pay and SSP may need to be considered in a situation where an employee is laid off by the employer whilst in a period of sickness and in receipt of SSP. In this context the employer's liability to pay a guarantee payment is not absolutely clear since to date this point has not been specifically tested by the courts. However, it is at least arguable that the right to receive SSP is implied into all eligible employees' contracts of employment, and therefore will act as a contractual payment which goes towards discharging the employer's liability for guarantee pay. On the other hand, it can be argued that, since entitlement to guarantee pay arises only on a day when an employee "would normally be required to work" under the contract, no entitlement arises when a worker is away sick.

Enforcement and Remedies

An employee may complain to an industrial tribunal that the employer has failed to pay the whole or any part of a guarantee payment due. Complaint must be made before the end of the period of three months beginning with the workless day, or within such further period as the tribunal considers reasonable in a case where it is satisfied that it was not reasonably practicable to present the complaint within three months.

If the tribunal finds that the complaint is well-founded it must order the employer to pay the employee the amount of the guarantee payment which it finds to be due.

The industrial tribunal has no power to compensate the employees for loss suffered by reason of the employer's failure to pay earlier.

Appendix 2 — Calculating Qualifying Service

The right to claim a redundancy payment and the right to claim unfair dismissals are determined for most employees by whether or not they can demonstrate the necessary qualifying service. The rules on calculating this service are contained in schedule 13 of the **Employment Protection (Consolidation) Act 1978** (EP(C)A). The rules cover five main areas:

- employment governed by a contract
- gaps in employment
- strikes and lock-outs
- change of employer
- reinstatement or re-engagement.

Employment Governed by a Contract

Until the House of Lords' ruling on 3 March 1994 employers could rely on the following qualifying provisions:

- 2 years' continuous employment under a contract which normally involves 16 hours or more per week
- 2 years' continuous employment under an arrangement that required the employee to work for at least 16 hours per week (ie the contract may state less than 16 hours, but the employee has always actually worked 16 hours or more)
- 5 years' continuous employment under a contract that normally involves 8 hours or more per week

- if the contractual hours are varied, and become a requirement to work at least 8 hours, these weeks will count towards continuous service, as long as the contractual hours revert to 16 or more per week within 26 weeks
- once qualifying service is acquired, employment protection is retained unless:
  (i) the contract is varied to fewer than 8 hours per week, and
  (ii) in any week the employee actually works for fewer than 16 hours.

The House of Lords ruled that these provisions are discriminatory as they treat part-timers less favourably, the majority of whom are women, and are therefore unlawful and in contravention of the EC Equal Pay Directive and the EC Equal Treatment Directive.

The **Employment Protection (Part-time Employees) Regulations 1995** have removed provisions which excluded employees from certain rights until they had completed 5 years' service if they work between 8 and 16 hours. This comes into effect from 6 February 1995.

Gaps in Employment, ie No Contract Existed

The employee was dismissed or resigned, and was subsequently re-employed.

The gap will count towards continuous service if the employee was:

(a) incapable of work due to sickness or injury
(b) absent from work on account of a temporary cessation of work
(c) absent from work in circumstances such that, by arrangement or custom, he or she is regarded as continuing in the employment of the employer for all or any purposes

(d) absent wholly or partly because of pregnancy or confinement (and not covered by the statutory maternity provisions (SMP)).

Conditions (a) and (d) are subject to the gap not exceeding a maximum of 26 weeks. Item (b) can often occur in redundancy situations where the employee is dismissed, and then the workload increases or the employer realises that too many employees were dismissed, and the employee is taken on again. Whether the gap breaks service can only be decided conclusively by a tribunal which will assess the length of the gap relative to the overall length of employment. Provision (c) covers continuing membership and contribution to a pension scheme and has been used successfully by staff employed under a series of fixed-term contracts, eg teachers.

Strikes and Lock-outs

Any day when an employee is on strike over terms and conditions of employment will not count towards continuous service. If the employee resumes work, irrespective of whether or not the contract was terminated during the strike, the service will be regarded as continuous, but the days the strike lasted must be deducted (ie the starting date of continuous employment is brought forward for the purposes of the calculation).

If the employee was locked out, then continuity is not broken and the days may well count because:

- the contract subsisted throughout the lock-out
- the contract was terminated, but the gap between dismissal and re-employment counts as a temporary cessation of work (see page 136).

If the locked out employee is dismissed and not re-employed, the lock-out days must be deducted from the period of continuous employment.

If employees on strike are dismissed and not re-employed, the question of continuous service will not arise and they may have lost the right to claim unfair dismissal, ie if the action was unofficial or the employer did not re-employ any of those taking part within three months of their dismissal.

Change of Employer

Service with a previous employer will count if:

- the employer changes due to a transfer of a trade, business or undertaking (ie the transfer falls within the TUPE regulations or under the EP(C)A schedule 13 definition)
- the employer dies and the employee is kept on or re-employed within eight weeks of the death by the deceased employer's personal representative or trustees
- there is a change in the partners, personal representatives or trustees
- the new employer is an associated employer, ie both companies are controlled by a third or one is controlled by the other.

Reinstatement or Re-engagement of Dismissed Employees

Employees dismissed and subsequently reinstated or re-engaged will have their continuity of employment preserved if the reinstatement or re-engagement occurred in the following circumstances:

- after a complaint of unfair dismissal or of unlawful sex or race discrimination arising from a dismissal has been presented to an industrial tribunal
- in response to the actions of an ACAS officer
- following the signing of a compromise agreement, in which the employee undertakes to refrain from instituting or continuing tribunal proceedings. TURERA 1993 contains the provisions for compromise agreements: they must be in writing and the employee must have received independent legal advice from a qualified

solicitor or barrister covered by professional indemnity insurance.

Appendix 3 — Exclusions from the Right to Claim Unfair Dismissal

Unless it is claimed that the dismissal was on grounds of sex, race, health and safety, trade union membership or activities or assertion of a statutory right, employees with less than two years' continuous employment are excluded.

Qualifying service is currently 2 years' continuous employment by the effective date of termination, regardless of the number of hours worked.

Other exclusions are as follows:

- the employee ordinarily works outside Great Britain
- the employment is under a fixed-term contract of one year or more, the contract contains a waiver clause and the dismissal consists only of the expiry of the fixed-term contract
- share fishermen and the police are excluded
- the employee is over the normal retiring age for the position held or, if no normal retiring age exists, has reached the age of 65
- the employee was dismissed whilst taking unofficial strike action or industrial action, *or* was dismissed whilst taking official strike action or other official industrial action and no-one dismissed has been reinstated or re-engaged within three months of the employees' dismissals
- the claim was not submitted to the tribunal within three months of the effective date of termination, and the tribunal does not grant an extension.

Appendix 4 — Interim Relief

When the employee claims that dismissal is principally on the grounds that the employee:

(a) was or proposed to become a member of a particular independent trade union

(b) had taken part, or proposed to take part, in the activities of an independent trade union at an appropriate time

(c) was not a member of any trade union, or a particular trade union, or had refused or proposed to refuse to become or remain a member

(d) was designated by the employer to carry out activities in connection with preventing or reducing risks to health and safety at work, and carried out, or proposed to carry out, any such activities

(e) was a representative on matters of health and safety at work or a member of a safety committee (either in accordance with arrangements established under or by virtue of any enactment, or by reason of being acknowledged as such by the employer) and performed or proposed to perform any such functions as a representative or member of such a committee

then the employee can apply to the tribunal for an order for interim relief. The application must be presented within seven days of the effective date of termination if the application is on the grounds of (a), (b) or (c), and within the same time limit an authorised union official must submit a certificate stating that there are reasonable grounds to believe that discrimination has occurred. The tribunal can order either reinstatement or re-engagement if it considers that there is a *prima facie* case.

If the employer is unwilling to comply or does not attend the interim relief hearing, or the employee reasonably refuses re-engagement, then the tribunal must make an order of the *continuation of the contract* until the complaint of unfair dismissal is settled or decided. This means, in effect, that the employee must receive normal pay and continuity is preserved.

Appendix 5 — Insolvency

When employment is terminated because the employer is insolvent, the employee may be able to recover any payments due. The relevant statutes in these circumstances are the **Insolvency Act 1986** and the **Employment Protection (Consolidation) Act 1978** (EP(C)A), as amended by the **Employment Act 1990**.

Provisions under the Insolvency Act

Some debts are paid out of the remaining assets before others, ie they are given preferential treatment. Included in these preferential payments are wages accrued in the four month period preceding the bankruptcy or liquidation. The maximum sum that can be accrued during this period, and receive preferential treatment, is currently £800. Any amounts in excess of this, or any debt of wages accrued prior to the four month period, will not receive preferential treatment and are classified as ordinary debts.

Wages, for the purposes of the Act, include:

- guarantee payments
- remuneration due to suspension on medical grounds
- time-off payments to trade union representatives for trade union duties and training
- time-off payments for ante-natal classes
- time-off payments due to employees under notice of redundancy in respect of time off to look for alternative work or to make arrangements for training.

These payments may be preferential, but they can only be paid if the assets are sufficient.

Under the provisions of the EP(C)A however, certain payments are guaranteed. The employee must apply in writing to the Secretary of State for Employment for settlement of these guarantee debts from the National Insurance Fund. These guaranteed debts are:

(a) up to eight weeks' arrears of pay (subject to the current maximum of £205 per week)

(b) payment for holidays taken or accrued

(c) compensation for unpaid statutory notice

(d) compensation for an unpaid basic award for unfair dismissal

(e) reimbursement of a fee or premium paid by an apprentice or articled clerk

(f) a "protective award" made by a tribunal for failure to consult with trade unions over redundancy.

The relevant date is:

- the date the employer became insolvent for payments (a) and (b)

- either the date of insolvency or the date of the award, whichever is the later, for payments (c) and (e)

- the date of insolvency, the date of termination of employment or the date of the award, whichever is the latest, for payments (d) and (f).

This means that redundant employees can claim from the National Insurance Fund irrespective of the prospects of the settlement of remaining debts, whether preferential or ordinary.

Insolvency, for the purposes of the EP(C)A, is defined as:

- liquidation, receivership, an administration order or a voluntary agreement if the employer is a company

- bankruptcy (sequestration in Scotland) or a special arrangement with creditors if the employer is an individual or a member of a partnership.

Exclusions

There are no length of service or age qualifications attached to the EP(C)A provisions, but certain employees are excluded:

- share fishermen
- merchant seamen
- employees who ordinarily work outside the territory of the Member States of the European Union
- Crown employees.

Remedy

Complaints that the Secretary of State has not made the payments due or that insufficient payment has been made must be presented to an industrial tribunal within three months of the refusal to pay or receipt of the part payment. If the tribunal upholds the claim, it will make a declaration and advise what payment is due.

Redundancy Payments

Employees entitled to statutory redundancy payments can apply to the Secretary of State for payment to be made out of the National Insurance Fund. This is dealt with under separate provisions of the EP(C)A. Disputes with the Secretary of State regarding the payments are made to an industrial tribunal. These provisions are fully explained in the Employment Department leaflet PL 718 Rev 1: *Employee's Rights on Insolvency of Employer*.

Appendix 6 — Notification to the Employment Department

Under s.193 of the **Trade Union and Labour Relations (Consolidation) Act 1992** (TULR(C)A) an employer proposing to make redundancies must give the Secretary of State for Employment advance notification whenever 10 or more employees are to be made redundant at one establishment. The notification must be given within certain time limits depending on the numbers being dismissed and the period over which the dismissals are to be effected.

The time limits are as follows:

(a) at least 90 days before the first dismissal takes effect if 100 or more employees are to be dismissed as redundant at one establishment over a period of 90 days or less

(b) at least 30 days before the first dismissal takes effect if 10–99 employees are to be dismissed as redundant at one establishment over a period of 30 days or less.

It is suggested that the notification, which must be given in writing, is made on Form HR1. This form is specifically designed for this purpose and is available from the Department of Employment. Ideally the form should be completed by the person responsible for administering the redundancy plan, for example a member of local management (usually the unit's personnel manager or personnel officer). Where redundancy is being effected in a number of company locations it is advisable to complete the form centrally, as redundancies from a number of units may need to be incorporated. This situation would arise where a business spread over various outlets is likely to be classed as one "establishment", meaning that redundancies at various locations should be counted together (see below).

Sections 1–6

These sections of the HR1 form require details to be entered of the employer's name and address and the name of the individual who should be contacted in connection with the notification.

Section 7

This requires details to be entered of the address of the establishment at which the employees to be made redundant are employed. For most employers these sections will normally create little difficulty. However, certain problems may arise in cases where redundancies occur at a number of locations since this gives rise to the question as to whether each separate outlet is to be classed as one "establishment" (reducing, potentially, the length of the notification period) for the purposes of the notification rules or whether they should all be categorised together as one business "establishment". Since the Act itself does not define "establishment" it has been left to the courts to determine this question on the facts of each particular case. In one case, a bakery and its associated retail shops comprised one establishment; in another a building headquarters and 14 sites all formed one establishment.

Section 8

This requires information on the nature of the business, for example retailer, banking, travel agent, etc.

Section 9

This section of the form provides boxes to be ticked detailing the main reasons for the redundancies. Each box is classified with a letter of the alphabet:

A: lower demand for products or services, B: completion of all or part of contract, C: transfer of activities to another workplace following a merger, D: transfer of activities to another workplace for other reasons, E: introduction of new plant or machinery, F: changes in work methods or organisation, G: introduction of new technology, H: something else.

The information detailed in this section of the form is important for the Department of Employment as it may have a bearing on whether the dismissals fall into the category of redundancy or whether they have been made for other reasons. For example, boxes C and G refer to situations where the transfer of business activities is the reason for the dismissals. These situations may be affected by the **Transfer of Undertakings Regulations** which provide that certain types of business transfer will not automatically create redundancy situations. Details of such situations are requested.

Sections 10 and 11

These sections of the form request information to be provided with regard to the numbers employed at the establishment in question and the numbers to be made redundant. The numbers to be dismissed will have a bearing on whether the employer has notified the Secretary of State within the correct time limit (see also *Sections 16 and 17*).

Sections 12–14

These sections ask for the composition of the workforce to be specified and request additional details about apprentices, trainees and young people.

Section 15

This requires the employer to state whether the entire establishment is to close.

Sections 16 and 17

To complete these the employer will need to specify the date the first proposed redundancy is planned to take place and the date on which the last redundancy will take effect. This information, combined with that in section 11, will enable the Department of Employment to see whether the HR1 has been submitted in due time.

Section 18

This section of the HR1 is concerned with the way in which the proposed redundancies are to be effected. Information is required on the basis on which employees are to be selected for redundancy. This would not be applicable in cases where, for example, the business was closing down and all employees were being dismissed. However, where selection does take place the method should be noted, ie whether this is based on length of service, "last in, first out", employees over normal retiring age, those with the poorest job performance, etc.

In effect these details are required by the Department of Employment "for information only". However, since the employer is also bound to provide a copy of the HR1 to recognised trade unions for categories of staff to be made redundant, this will serve the further purpose of informing the unions of the proposed selection procedures.

Sections 19–22

These provide for the employer to enter details of the unions concerned and to list the dates on which consultations began (s.188 of the TULR(C)A as amended requires employers to consult with recognised trade unions with a view to reaching agreement when redundancies are to be made). Where agreement has already been reached, this should be noted.

Finally, the form must be signed certifying that the information detailed is correct.

Where employers have failed to comply with the notification rules they may be fined on conviction. However, if the employers can show that there were special reasons rendering it not reasonably practicable to have complied with the requirements and that they had done all they could to meet the requirements, this will be considered a valid defence. In practice this means that employers should ideally send a letter accompanying form HR1 setting out clearly the reasons for non-compliance and, in effect, outlining their case as to why they should not be subject to legal proceedings.

Appendix 7 — Time Off

Some employees, once served with formal notice of dismissal on the grounds of redundancy, will have a statutory right to reasonable time off, by virtue of s.31(1) and (2) of the **Employment Protection (Consolidation) Act 1978** (EP(C)A). This entitlement covers time off to:

(a) look for new employment

(b) make arrangements for training.

There is a qualifying requirement of two years' continuous employment (regardless of the number of hours worked). The service is calculated up to and including the date the notice expires, or if notice was less than the statutory minimum entitlement, the date the statutory notice would have expired.

Time off is paid at the appropriate hourly rate, subject to a maximum of two-fifths of a week's pay (there is no financial limit on a week's pay) per notice period. The hourly rate is defined as a week's pay divided by either:

- the number of normal working hours stated on the contract, *or*
- if hours vary from week to week, the total number of hours worked during the 12 week period ending with the last complete week before the day on which notice was given, divided by 12.

The Legal Remedy

A complaint can be made to an industrial tribunal that the employer unreasonably refused time off on a particular day or refused to pay the amount due. The complaint must be made within three months of the day in question, although this limit can be extended if the tribunal considers it was not reasonably practicable to present the complaint within three months. If the complaint is well-founded, the tribunal must make a declaration and order the employer to pay the amount due (subject to a maximum of two-fifths of a week's pay).

Further Information

Could you use Additional Copies of this Book?

Croner's Guide to Managing Redundancy is a pocket book designed for practical use by all those with management responsibilities. If you are a subscriber to *Croner's Reference Book for Employers* this is one of a series of books on key areas of employment.

Are there other managers in your organisation who would benefit from having a copy to hand? If so, why not give them a copy to help them consolidate their knowledge and put into practice what they have learnt.

Additional copies at a special price of £6 plus £1 p+p per copy may be ordered by telephoning our Customer Services team on 0181-547 3333 quoting reference MGHQ.

Other Books

You may not be aware of the many books we publish on subjects of interest and relevance to employers. The broad range of topics covered reflects the breadth of your responsibilities and interests.

Our books always take a practical approach and are written with the non-specialist in mind. Jargon-free language, the essential facts and a clear format ensure that these books meet your needs.

Here are some of the titles we publish:

Introduction to Employment Law by Robert Upex, price: £19.95, ISBN: 1 85452 063 6

Protecting your Business and Confidential Information by Audrey Williams, price: £10.95, ISBN: 1 85524 109 9

Procedure in Industrial Tribunal Cases by Vivian Du-Feu, price: £12.95, ISBN: 1 85525 108 0

Collective Labour Law by Martin Warren, price: £10.95, ISBN: 1 85524 107 2

Psychometric Testing in Personnel Selection and Appraisal by Paul Kline, price: £19.95, ISBN: 1 85524 112 9

The Role of the Pension Fund Trustee by John Cunliffe, price: £15.95, ISBN: 1 85524 091 2

Debt Recovery in the County Court by Michael Barry, price: £19.95, ISBN: 1 85524 118 8

Dictionary of Payroll Terms by Derek French, price: £14.95, ISBN: 1 85524 162 5

A Guide to Fleet Management and Company Cars by Les Cheesman and Anthony Minns, price: £14.95, ISBN: 1 85524 119 6

For further details contact our Customer Services team on 0181-547 3333 quoting reference WBMD.

Conferences and Training

Attending a seminar is one of the best ways of keeping up with rapidly changing legislation, trends and new ideas. Croner Conferences and Training has 10 years' experience of running an extensive range of courses, from three-day residential to one-day seminars, all led by authoritative and experienced speakers.

Courses are regularly offered on the following subjects:

Handling Disciplinary Situations and Interviews
The Effective Secretary
Going to Tribunal
Concise Guide to Employment Law
Drafting Contracts of Employment
Managing Absenteeism
Statutory Sick Pay

SMP and Other Maternity Rights
The Effective Personnel Assistant
Introduction to Employment Law
Fair Dismissal — The "Dos and Don'ts"
Employment Law — The European Dimension
Drafting Contracts of Employment
Managing People Effectively
Selection Interviewing
Managing Performance Appraisal
Fleet Management
Smoking Policies
Company Secretary's Workshop
Occupational Pensions: Current Issues and Choices
Pension Fund Trustees Briefing
Developments in Payroll Management
VAT: A Basic Guide
VAT Inspectors and How to Deal with Them
PAYE Workshop
Payroll Management

For further information on any of these courses please contact Conferences and Training on 0181-547 3333 quoting reference VFFZ.

Croner In-Company Training offers courses on:

Employment Law
Management Skills
Health and Safety
Dangerous Substances
Importing/Exporting
VAT and Finance

… and many more tailored to your needs, for all levels of staff, anywhere in Europe.

Our packages comprise:

- participative, tailored courses
- no obligation preliminary meeting

- full back-up documentation
- experienced and practical trainers
- competitive price, estimated in advance
- backed up by the Croner reputation.

For details of value for money, affordable courses for four or more staff, tailored to your needs, ring Claire Spraggs on 0181-547 3333, quoting reference VFFZ.

Index

Please note the following:
1. Index entries are to page numbers.
2. Entries in italic relate to legal cases, forms, checklists and titles of publications.
3. Alphabetical arrangement is word-by-word, where a group of letters followed by a space is filed before the same group of letters followed by a letter, eg "in the" comes before "incentive".

A

ACAS (Advisory, Conciliation and Arbitration Service),
    addresses 127–128
additional awards 80, 82
addresses 127–130
advertising, for volunteers 87
age, for calculating redundancy pay 98, 107
agreed procedures, breaches of 62–65
appeals procedures 69
apprenticeships, completion of 41
associated employers 47–48
    defined 119
Association of University Teachers v University of Newcastle
[1988] IRLR 10 54
attendance records 66
awards, financial 80–83

B

B L Cars Ltd v Lewis [1983] IRLR 58 66
basic awards 80, 81
Bass Leisure Ltd v Thomas [1994] IRLR 8 49
Birch and Humber v University of Liverpool [1985] IRLR 165 ... 40
British Association of Counselling, address 128
Bromby and Hoare v Evans [1972] ICR 113 51
Brook v London Borough of Haringey [1992] IRLR 478 .... 66, 67
bumping *see* redundancy, transferred

businesses
    closures 47–49
    defined 119
    ownership, transfer of 37–40
    performance, linking pay to 15
    reviewing 9–12
    selling 12–13
buy-outs *see* management buy-outs

C

Cambridge and District Co-Op Society Ltd v Ruse [1993] IRLR
    156 103
Carry all Motors Law v Pennington [1980] IRLR 455 51
Checklist: A guide to Meaningful Consultation 77
Checklist: The information needed for calculating
    the payment due 108
collective agreements
    claims of discrimination with 68
    defined 119–120
compensatory awards 80, 81–82
conferences 158–160
constructive dismissals 33–34
consultations
    importance of 75–79
    with non-unionised employees 26–27
    with the individual employee 73–75
    with trade unions 23–26
continuous employment 107–108
continuous service 98
contract work, offering 88
contracts
    fixed term, expiry of 30–32, 41, 98–99
    of employment, defined 120
    terminations of, that do not qualify for
        redundancy pay 37–43
contractual provision 19–20
contractual remuneration 133
core staffing 7–8
Cowen v Haden Carrier Ltd [1982] IRLR 255 64

Croner's Reference Book for Employers..22
Croydon Advertiser Group v Clinton 468/91............................76
customary arrangements, breaches of................................62–65

D

Delanair Ltd v Mead [1976] IRLR 340 51
Denton v Neepsend Ltd [1976] IRLR 164.....................................52
Department of Employment
    addresses...129–130
    notification of redundancies...................................27, 149–153
    role in helping unemployed 93–94
Deregulation Bill...69
disciplinary warnings..66
discrimination, in selection..67, 68
dismissals
    constructive 33–34
    defining 29–43
    during trial period 104–105
    inadmissible reasons for...58–65
    unfair
        exclusions from the right to claim 141–142
        legal remedies for 80–83
Duffy v Yeomans and Partners Ltd [1993] IRLR 368.....................74

E

EC Collective Redundancies Directive 75/129 25
education *see* further education
effective date of termination, defined......................................120
employees
    defined...120
    helping...92–95
    resignations during notice..35–37
Employee's Rights on Insolvency of Employer (Dept of
    Employment leaflet, PL718 Rev 1).....................................147
employers
    changes of 138
    defined...120
employment
    see also self employment; unemployment

alternative..77–79, 83–84, 101–105
continuous.. 107–108
contract of, defined 120
defined 120–121
Department of *see* Department of Employment
gaps in... 98, 136–137
governed by a contract.. 135–136
outside Great Britain..99
Employment Protection (Consolidation)
Act 1978 (EP(C)A) 19, 30, 45, 57, 98, 135, 145, 155
Employment Protection (Part-time Employees) Regulations
1995...136
Equal Pay Act 1970...33
express terms.. 19, 32–33
extended trial periods... 103–104

F

fair selection, establishing 57–71
Ferguson v Prestwick Circuits Ltd [1992] IRLR 266 76
fixed-term contracts, expiry of 30–32, 41, 98–99
Frame It v Brown [1993] EAT 177/93 51
further education..91

G

Gillies v Richard Daniels and Co Ltd [1979] IRLR 457 33
glossary 119–125
guarantee payments................................... 20–22, 131–134

H

Hartwell Commercial group Ltd v Brand and Jones
EAT 506/92 55
Hempell v W H Smith and Sons Ltd [1986] IRLR 95 105
Henry v Ellerman City Liners Ltd [1984] IRLR 409 63
Hindes v Supersine Ltd [1979] IRLR 343....................................102
holidays, bringing forward 14
hours, reducing 15

I

implied terms ....19, 33 "in the place" *see* place of work

incentive terms 88

independent trade union, defined 121

industrial action *see* strikes

Industrial Relations Code of Practice 73–74

Industrial Tribunals (Central Offices), addresses................... 130

information, further.. 157–160

insolvency 145–147

Insolvency Act 1986 145

interim relief 143–144

Ionising Radiations Regulations 1985.. 61

J

James v Eastleigh Borough Council [1990] IRLR 288 67

job

    defined.. 121

    performance, contribution to business 67

    sharing.. 16–17

Johnson and Dutton v Notts Combined Policy Authority
    [1974] IRLR 20 .... 52, 54

Jones v Association Tunnelling Co. Ltd [1981] IRLR 477 49

L

labour costs, reducing 13–17

lay-offs 19–22

Lee v Notts County Council [1980] IRLR 284............................ 30

LIFO (last in, first out).............................63–64, 65–66, 67

Lignacite Products Ltd v Krollman [1979] IRLR 23 100

Litster and Others v Forth Dry Dock and Engineering Co
    [1989] IRLR 161 39–40

lock-outs 137–138

M

MacFisheries Ltd v Findlay and Others [1985] ICR 160............... 52

management buy-outs 13

manpower planning... 5–7

Marshall v Harland and Wolff Ltd and Another
    [1972] IRLR 90 53

maternity leave, failure to allow return from...................... 34–35

Maund v Penrith District Council [1984] IRLR 24 54
Melon v Hector Powe Ltd [1980] IRLR 479 38
Mining Supplies (Longwall) Ltd v Baker [1988] IRLR 417 75
misconduct 99–100
month, defined 121
Morton Sundour Fabrics Ltd v Shaw [1966] ITR 84 30
Mulrine v University of Ulster [1993] IRLR 547 32
multiple trial periods 104
Murphy v Epsom College [1985] ICR 80 52
mutual agreements, of termination of employment 40–41

N

Nelson v BBC [1977] IRLR 148 52
notice
    of extension 100–101
    of termination of employment 30
notifications of redundancies
    to the Department of Employment 149–153
    to the Press 92

O

obligatory periods 35–36
offer of re-engagement, defined 121
official, defined 121–122
Offsetting pensions against redundancy payments (Dept of
    Employment leaflet, RLP1) 111
Open University v Triesman [1978] IRLR 114 32
operation of law, dismissal by 37
outplacement assistance 94–95

P

part-time work 16
pay
    linking to business performance 15
    redundancy, calculation of 105–112
payments *see* guarantee payments; redundancy payments
penalties, for failing to meet consultation
    requirements 25–26
pensions, offsetting 111–112

Philip Hodges & Co v Kell [1994] IRLR 569 79
Pink v I White and Z white and Co (Earls Barton) Ltd
  [1985] IRLR 489 .... 53, 64
place of work 48–49
Polkey v A E Dayton Services [1987] IRLR 503 .... 69, 74–77
pool of selection 64–65
position, defined 122
procedures
  agreed 62–65
  appeal 69
  redundancy, reasonable 73–85
Purdy v Willowbrook International Ltd [1977] IRLR 388 21

Q

qualifying service, calculating 135–139

R

Race Relations Act 82
Rank Xerox Ltd v Churchill and Others [1988] IRLR 280 48
Redmond Stichting, Dr Sophie, v Bartol and Others
  [1992] IRLR 366 39
re-engagement
  of dismissed employees.. 138–139
  offer of, defined... 121
  under new contract 41
recognised trade union, defined.. 122
record keeping.. 79
Red Bank Manufacturing Co Ltd v Meadows [1992] IRLR 209 ... 75
redundancy
  avoiding 5–17
  defining 45–55
  minimising the impact of 87–95
  notifications of... 92, 149–153
  payments... 97–117
    and employer insolvency...................................... 147
    dismissals that qualify for................................ 35–37
    entitlement to 21–22
    terminations of contracts that do not qualify for 37–43
  reasonable procedure for.. 73–85

transferred..48, 79
unfair..53–55
Redundancy Handling (ACAS guidance booklet) 65, 73
Redundancy Payments Act 1965...97
Redundancy Payments Pensions Regulations 1965...............111
Redundancy Selection Assessment Form 71
reinstatement.. 80, 138–139
relevant date
   defined..122
   for calculating redundancy pay................................. 106–107
renewal
   defined..122
   of contract..41
resignations
   by employees during notice.......................................35–37
   during trial period 104
retirement, early...89–91
retraining *see* training
Robinson v British Island Airways Ltd [1977] IRLR 477 52
Rolls Royce Motor Cars Ltd v Price and Others EAT
   [1993] IRLR 203...68

S

sabbaticals...92
Sanders and others v Ernest A Neale Ltd [1974] IRLR 236 54
Scott and others v Coalite Fuels and Chemicals Ltd
   [1988] IRLR 131...41
Secretary of State for Employment v Spence and Others
   [1986] IRLR 248...39
selection, establishing fair 57–71
self-employment...88–89
Sex Discrimination Act 1986 ....68, 82
short-time working 19–22
special awards.. 80, 82–83
Spencer and Griffen v Gloucs County Council
   [1985] IRLR 393...103
staffing *see* core staffing
statutory payments 133
statutory sick pay (SSP) 134

statutory trial periods... 103
STC Ltd v Yates [1981] IRLR 21 102
strikes...100–101, 137–138
    defined.. 123
successor, defined 123
Suflex Ltd v Thomas and Others [1978] IRLR 435....................... 63

T

Tayside Health Board v Doogan EAT 226/93 63
termination
    effective date of, defined 120
    of contracts that do not qualify for redundancy
        payments 37–43
terms
    express.. 19, 32–33
    implied 19, 33
    incentive.. 88
Thomas and Betts Manufacturing Co Ltd v Harding
    [1978] IRLR 213 ....58, 63
time keeping 66
time off 155–156
timing, of consultations.. 25
trade dispute, defined 123–124
Trade Union and Labour Relations (Consolidation)
    Act 1992 (TULR(C)A)...23, 59, 149
Trade Union Reform and Employment Rights Act 1993
    (TURERA) 38, 58
trade unions
    consulting with 23–27
    defined.. 124
    dismissal on grounds of.. 59–62
    independent, defined 121
    recognised, defined 122
training
    courses.. 158–160
    for other work 91
Transfer of Undertakings Regulations 1981, SI 1981
    No. 1794 (TUPE) 12–13, 37, 47, 151
transferred redundancy 79

transfers
    effects on employees' contracts...39–40
    of business ownership...37–39
trial periods 84–85, 103–105
TULR(C)A *see* Trade Union and Labour Relations
    (Consolidation) Act 1992
TUPE *see* Transfer of Undertakings Regulations 1981 (SI No.
    1981 No. 1794)
TURERA *see* Trade Union Reform and Employment Rights
    Act 1993

U

UK Security Services (Midlands) Ltd v Gibbons and Others
    EAT 104/90 40
undertakings, definition of 57–58
unemployment, alternatives to 81–95

V

volunteers
    encouraging 87–91
    for part-time work 16

W

W Gimber and Sons Ltd v Spurrett [1967] ITR 308 79
Wages Act 1986 ....20, 60, 97
wages, reduction in 14–15
waiver clauses 31–32
Wall's Meat Co Ltd v Selby..73
warnings *see* disciplinary warnings
week, defined 19, 109, 125
week's pay, calculating 108–112
Western Excavating (ECC) Ltd v Sharp [1978] IRLR 27 32
Williams and Others v Compair Maxam Ltd [1982]
    IRLR 83...65, 68
"work of a particular kind" 50–53

Y

year, defined 125